edited by Hoikusha
Publishing Co., Ltd.

translated by
Don Kenny

CONTENTS

Traditional Japan . . . 1	Japan Today 44
Gardens 6	Tokyo 46
Architecture 10	Nikkô 58
Swords 14	Kamakura 62
Pottery 14	Mount Fuji, Hakone,
Makie 15	Izu 65
Painting 18	Kyoto 70
Ikebana 20	Mount Hiei and
Calligraphy 22	Lake Biwa 75
Chanoyu 24	Nara 78
Kabuki 30	Osaka 82
Noh 30	Kôbe 86
Bunraku 30	Hiroshima 87
Buyô 31	The Seto Inland
Matsuri 34	Sea 89
Japanese Dolls 36	Kyûshû 90
Martial Arts 38	The Japan Alps 93
Cuisine 40	Hokkaidô 94
Dwarfed Trees 43	The Land of Japan . . 98
Miniature Landscapes . 43	The Flow of Japanese
Goldfish 43	Culture 103

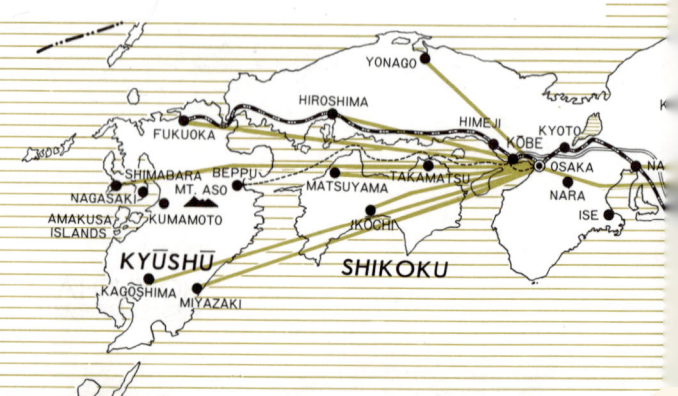

Hokusai / Mt. Fuji Scenes off Kanagawa

Japan is beautiful. Natural beauty is apparent everywhere, as well as the beauty of the culture – her traditional arts, which have been created and developed by her people over the last two thousand years. Sometimes Japanese arts are difficult to understand because of their subtle, underlying meanings and purposes, but the more one learns about the history and culture, the more fascinated one becomes, and the more one learns to appreciate the country and its people.

In the following pages, I have attempted to explain the flow of cultural history, to help the reader gain an understanding of the arts, customs, and people of Japan.

References to periods in Japanese history will appear often in these pages. Here is a chronological list, with the corresponding dates in the Western calendar:

(Cover Photo) Heian Shrine in Kyoto

JAPAN

translated by Don Kenny

© All rights reserved. No.17 of Hoikusha's Color Books Series. Published by Hoikusha Publishing Co., Ltd., 6-12, 1-chome, Kawamata, Higashiosaka, 577-0063 Japan. ISBN 4-586-54017-6. First Edition in 1969. 41st Edition in 1998. Printed in JAPAN.

TRADITIONAL JAPAN

Aoi Matsuri (The Festival of the Hollyhock) —Kyoto—

Hokusai / Mt. Fuji Scenes off Kanagawa

Japan is beautiful. Natural beauty is apparent everywhere, as well as the beauty of the culture — her traditional arts, which have been created and developed by her people over the last two thousand years. Sometimes Japanese arts are difficult to understand because of their subtle, underlying meanings and purposes, but the more one learns about the history and culture, the more fascinated one becomes, and the more one learns to appreciate the country and its people.

In the following pages, I have attempted to explain the flow of cultural history, to help the reader gain an understanding of the arts, customs, and people of Japan.

References to periods in Japanese history will appear often in these pages. Here is a chronological list, with the corresponding dates in the Western calendar:

Asuka period	middle of 6c.— 710
Nara period	710 — 794
Heian period	794 — 1192
Kamakura period	1192 — 1333
Nanbokuchō period	1333 — 1392
Muromachi period	1392 — 1573
[Sengoku period	1467 — 1568]
Azuchi Momoyama period	1573 — 1603
Edo period	1603 — 1868
Meiji period	1868 — 1912
Taisho period	1912 — 1926
Showa period	1926 — 1989
Heisei period	1989 —

Sōtatsu / The Wind-imp

Stone Garden of Ryōan-ji —Kyoto—

Garden of Saihō-ji (Moss Temple) —Kyoto—

Garden of Ginkaku-ji —Kyoto—

GARDENS

Japanese gardens are generally divided into two general classifications — the pond and plant type, and the rock and sand type. There are pond and plant gardens which are made to be walked through and those which are made to be viewed from a verandah.

During the Asuka and Nara periods (588 – 793), Buddhist culture was introduced into Japan. Along with it came gardening techniques and aesthetics. Gardens came to be built as symbols of paradise.

During the Heian period (794 –1184), the *shinden* style of architecture came into vogue, and along with it, spacious gardens with ponds large enough for boating.

Along with the rise of the military class during the Kamakura period (1185–1333), the *buke-shoin* style of architecture gained popularity over the aristocratic *shinden* style. Zen Buddhism became the religion of the day, and along with it gardens made to walk through began to appear. A representative of this type of garden can be seen at the Saihō-ji in Kyoto.

The Muromachi period (1394 –1466) was the time when the extremely abbreviated symbolism of the rock and sand gardens came into being. The garden at the Ryōan-ji in Kyoto is a particularly well-known example of this style.

Tea gardens appeared at the height of Momoyama culture (latter half of the 16th century) in the gorgeous style with stone bridges and groves of carefully trimmed trees and bushes.

The Edo period (1603 – 1867) saw the perfection of all the previous styles and a combination of all their elements to form natural miniature landscapes and reproductions of famous scenes.

With the introduction of Western culture, Western gardens also became popular in Japan.

(See HOIKUSHA COLOR BOOKS 9 Kyoto Gardens.)

Garden of Daisen-in —Kyoto—

Katsura Imperial Villa —Kyoto—

Himeji Castle —Himeji— ▶

Ise Shrine —Ise, Mie Prefecture—

ARCHITECTURE

Japan has always had a rich natural supply of lumber, resulting in the development of almost exclusively wooden architecture up until the Meiji period.

The oldest and most truly Japanese form of architecture is found in the ancient Shinto temples, the best examples of which are Ise Shrine, the Grand Izumo Shrine, and Sumiyoshi Shrine. The three styles seen in these temples have a history dating back more than 2,000 years.

Buddhist culture was introduced into Japan during the Nara period. Along with the philosophy came Buddhist architecture, good examples of which are the Hōryu-ji and the Tōdai-ji in Nara. The main hall of the Tōdai-ji is well-known as the largest wooden structure in the world. Changes in architectural style were introduced later, along with the rise in popularity of Jōdo, Zen, and other sects of Buddhism.

Hōryu-ji —Nara Prefecture—

Dwellings of the aristocrats during the Heian period were built in a symmetrical style known as *shinden-zukuri*. During the Muromachi and Momoyama periods, the *shinden-zukuri* style was rearranged logically and improved upon, producing a new, more practical style of architecture called *shoin-zukuri*, of which the Katsura Imperial Villa is an excellent example. Further developments led into the *sukiya-zukuri*, found in the dwellings and tea houses of the Edo period, which is the basis of modern Japanese dwelling house architecture. (See HOIKUSHA COLOR BOOKS 1 Katsura).

Castle architecture developed separately beginning with simple fortresses during the early part of the middle ages, and later, when the daimyo became the political and financial leaders of society, became gorgeous mansions. (See HOIKUSHA COLOR BOOKS 12 Japanese Castles.)

P. 12 The Shaka triad, main image of the Kondō, Hōryū-ji (Nara)
P. 13 The Kichijō-ten image, Jōruri-ji (Kyoto)

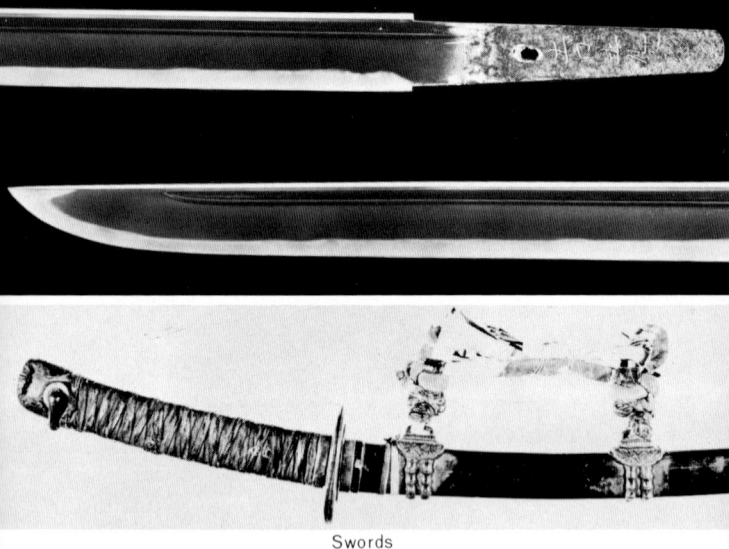
Swords

SWORDS

Early swords were imported from China, but during the Heian period, iron ore was discovered in Japan, sword making techniques were developed, and the Japanese sword was born. During the days of the warrior social system, the sword was considered the very spirit of the warrior himself. During the Edo period, decorations were devised, raising the sword to a work of high quality art, and the Japanese sword became famous throughout the world.

POTTERY

Japanese pottery includes ceramics and porcelain. Porcelain was introduced into Japan during the Kamakura and Muromachi periods. Among Japanese porcelains, best-known are Arita, Seto, Kutani, and Kiyomizu. Ceramics have also been produced in Japan since the Kamakura period, mainly at Seto in Aichi prefecture. The most important Japanese ceramic product is the bowl used in the Tea Ceremony.

Pottery

Makie

MAKIE

The technique of embedding gold, silver, and mother-of-pearl patterns in lacquer to produce practical and decorative household utensils was developed in Japan, beginning in the Nara period, and reached its zenith during the Heian period, in beautiful ink and letter boxes.

Genji Monogatari Emaki (Tale of Genji Scrolls)

"Tree Peony" in Daikaku-ji —Kyoto—

Sketch style of Ōkyo

New *Yamato-e* style of Kōrin

PAINTING

The history of Japanese painting begins in the Heian period. The two earliest styles were called *kara-e* and *Yamato-e*. *Kara-e* refers to the style imported from China, and *Yamato-e*, the style developed in Japan. In contrast to the strong, aggressive effect of Buddhist painting, the delicate beauty of the long scroll paintings called *emaki-mono* were products of and deeply expressive of the life and culture of Heian period aristocrats.

Ukiyo-e woodblock print of Utamaro

During the Muromachi period, the Zen Buddhist ink painting style became a great influence on the art world of Japan. Under its influence, the Kano school was born and dominated Japanese art from the Momoyama period and into the Edo period. The style of the Kano school is a wedding of the Zen ink painting style and the *Yamoto-e*.

The Kano school was strong throughout the Edo period with the upper classes, but with the rise of the merchant class, such new popular art forms as the New *Yamato-e* style of Kōrin, the *Ukiyo-e* woodblock prints of Utamaro and others, and the sketch style of Ōkyo, as well as Western arts forms, made their influence felt. (See HOIKUSHA COLOR BOOKS 2 Tokaido, 3 Emaki and 5 Ukiyoe.)

A traditional Ikebana is arranged in the Tokonoma.

Arrangement of flowers in a vase for the purpose of viewing for pleasure or offering to a god has always been practiced, not only in Japan, but in all other countries of the world as well. The main difference between Japanese IKEBANA and flower arrangement of other cultures is that in IKEBANA, the arranger approaches his work as an expressive artist. (See HOIKUSHA COLOR BOOKS 10 Ikebana)

IKEBANA

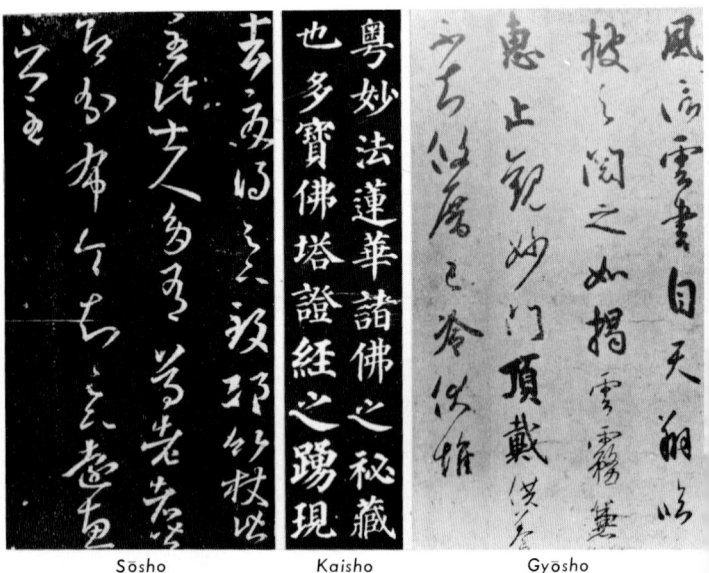

Sōsho　　　Kaisho　　　Gyōsho

CALLIGRAPHY

Japanese calligraphy, known as *shodo* is an ancient art in which the writing of Chinese characters (*kanji*) and Japanese syllabary (*kana*) is accomplished with India ink (*sumi*) and a special soft brush. It was introduced along with the *kanji* from China very early, and by the early part of the Heian period, it had been developed into a distinctive Japanese art form. The three basic styles of writing are *kaisho, gyōsho,* and *sōsho*. Recently, avant garde and abstract styles have been developed and gained great popularity.

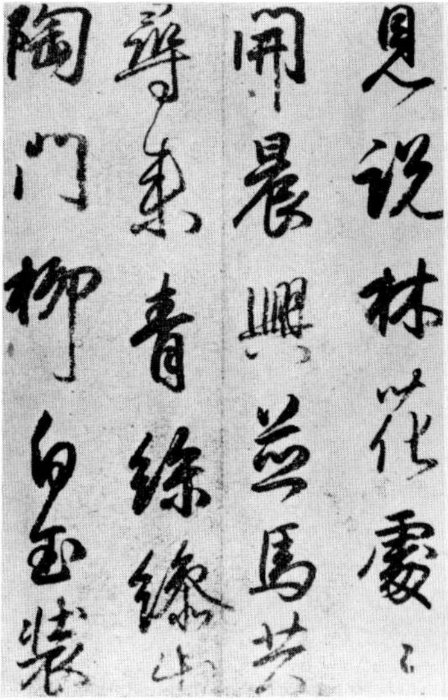

| Gyōsho | Sōsho |

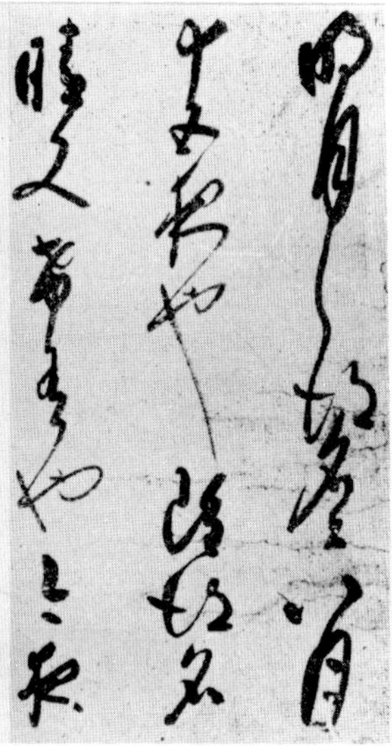

Avant garde and abstract style

23

CHANOYU

The Tea Ceremony, which is called CHANOYU in Japanese, is the art of drinking a bitter tea made of lightly ground, dried tea leaves, called *matcha*. The ground leaves are placed in a bowl or large tea cup, boiling water is poured over them, and the mixture is whipped into a foam with a bamboo tea whisk.

The real purpose of this ceremonial drinking of tea is to relax the mind, and make it open to appreciate the surrounding beauty, and to communicate with those present, on a higher artistic, more intellectual, and more peaceful level.

Tea cup (Chawan)

Tea caddy (Natsume)

Tea Ceremony in the Shoin

The ceremonial drinking of tea was originally imported from China, but as all other importations, it was thoroughly assimilated and transformed into something truly Japanese. It has been practiced in its present form in Japan for approximately 400 years. It is a total art, which places equal demands on the concentration of heart and mind as on the stylization of movement and formalization of the behavior of the participants.

Tea Ceremony was originally the simple practice of the priest in Buddhist temples of offering tea, which had been donated, to worshippers in front of the altar in their temples, upon which were arranged sacred flowers.

During the latter half of the 14th century, a man named Murata Shukō began preaching the idea that the same respectful attitude and highly artistic surroundings were appropriate for entertaining guests in one's own house. He brought about reforms in the construction of tea houses, and the use and selection of utensils used. Later the art was perfected by Sen no Rikyū, who set up rules covering all aspects, from construction of the tea house in the *sukiya* style, to flower arrangement, decoration of the room, arrangement and use of utensils, and the qualifications necessary for a true tea master. Through the centuries slight variations in interpretation of Rikyū's precepts have resulted in the formation of various "schools", but the basic spirit of the Tea Ceremony today is that of Rikyū, its perfector. (See HOIKUSHA COLOR BOOKS 31 Tea Ceremony.)

Tea Ceremony

Noh

◀ Kabuki

Bunraku

KABUKI

Kabuki was born and developed during the Edo period as the theater of the people. Okuni with her troupe of Dancing temple maidens presented their first performances of the Buddhist *Nembutsu-odori* and Okuni's original *Kabuki-odori* in Kyoto in 1603. Beginning around 1653, the dramatic, as opposed to the revue-type aspects were developed and the art was brought to its zenith during the last part of the 18th and beginning of the 19th centuries. Kabuki is basically a drama of music and dance. Its special styles of dialogue delivery and movement demand a high musical sense, and an overall pictorial beauty is stressed. (See HOIKUSHA COLOR BOOKS 11 Kabuki.)

NOH

Noh is one of Japan's oldest classical stage arts. It is a masked drama, which stresses highly refined beauty in sound and dance movement. It originated in the *sarugaku*, which was popular along with the older rice planting song and dance called *dengaku*, during the Heian period. During the Muromachi period, it reached its zenith in a form similar to the form we know today. Noh was originally presented outdoors in a grassy area. The Noh stage came into being during the Momoyama period. (See HOIKUSHA COLOR BOOKS 15 Noh.)

BUNRAKU

Bunraku, also called puppet *jōruri*, is a style of drama in which puppets are handled to the accompaniment of the *shamisen* and a narrator. Along with Noh and Kabuki, Bunraku is one of the three great classical stage arts of Japan.

Puppets originated in religious ceremonies, and became popular as a form of public entertainment around the 11th century. Puppet shows became extremely popular during the 15th and 16th centuries, and into the 17th century, during which the *shamisen* accompaniment and narrators were added to form the art known today as Bunraku.

Japanese classical dance "Musume Dōjōji"

BUYO

Buyo is the general term used to refer to the whole field of Japanese classical dance, which is loosely divided into two general styles – Kabuki dance, and the chamber dance style called *jiuta-mai*.

Kabuki dance was develop mainly in Edo, and is performed as part of a Kabuki program, accompanied by various styles of song and narration such as *nagauta, tokiwazu, kiyomoto,* and *gidayu-bushi*.

Jiuta-mai, on the other hand, was developed from the Noh dances, in the Osaka-Kyoto area, as a chamber dance style, with *jiuta* as its accompaniment. It is very subdued, with only very small, delicate movements, and a deep inner strength as its main characteristics.

Gion Matsuri (Gion Festival)
—Kyoto—

Fire Festival at Mt. Wakakusa —Nara—

Namahage (Devil Festival) of Akita Prefecture

MATSURI

Japanese folk festivals, called MATSURI, originated in the primitive religious beliefs of the common people and are still very much a part of life in the provinces. Various decorations, performances, and rituals make up the endless variety of expressions of belief and prayer throughout Japan. (See HOIKUSHA COLOR BOOKS 13 Japanese Festivals.)

Sanja Festival of Asakusa Shrine in Tokyo

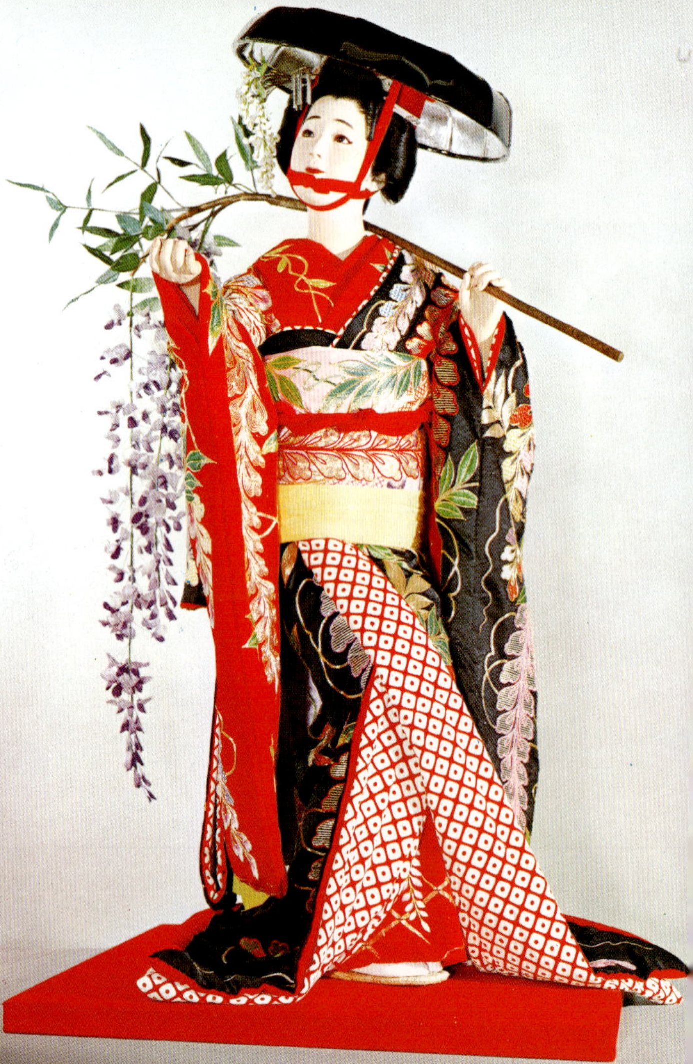

Japanese dolls

◀ Japanese doll

37

Kendō

MARTIAL ARTS

Kendō is the art of Japanese swordsmanship. The body is protected by a mask, arm padding, and a chest plate. A bamboo sword is used in place of a real weapon during the training period.

Jūdō is a self defense art in which no weapons are used. It is a system of punches, kicks, throws, and holds by which one subdues one's opponent. Jūdō was organized into a logical system in 1882, and since that time has gained great popularity throughout the world.

Sumō wrestling is the Japanese national sport. It dates back to the ancient mythology of the creation of Japan. Professional wrestlers first appeared during the Edo period, and since that time it has entered the realm of spectator sports rather than the martial arts. The point of the match is to either throw one's opponent down or out of the ring.

Jūdō

Sumō

CUISINE

Sukiyaki is known by gourmets the world over. A deep iron skillet is set over a fire in the middle of the table, thinly cut beef and various vegetables are fried in a sauce of sugar and soy sauce.

Tempura is said to have been introduced into Japan from Portugal during the Muromachi period. Fresh fish and vegetables are dipped in a thick batter of flour and egg, then deep fat fried, and eaten with various relishes and dips.

Kaiseki-ryori is the name for the formal Japanese dining style. It originated with the Tea Ceremony during the Muromachi period. During the Edo period, it became more elaborate, *sake* took the place of tea as the main beverage, and it has come down to us today in its present grand banquet form.

Dwarfed Trees

Miniature Landscapes

Goldfish

DWARFED TREES
MINIATURE LANDSCAPES
GOLDFISH

Dwarfed trees called *bonsai* became popular during the Kamakura period. The art has continue to develop through the centuries, and is still popular today.

Miniature landscapes, known as *suiseki,* express the beauties of nature with a single stone or group of small stones as the central point of interest. This art dates back to the latter part of the Muromachi period. Recent developments have broadened the range of expression to include shapes of animals and human beings.

Goldfish *(kingyo)* were bred from the carp family over 2000 years ago in China. The raising of goldfish became popular in Japan around 1700 A.D. Many varieties have been developed in Japan, and today goldfish are an important export product.

JAPAN TODAY

Japan's new entranceway of the skies was opened on May 20, 1978. At present regular flights of 34 airlines from 31 nations provide 175 to 180 flights a day in and out of Japan from Narita. During the primary stage of construction, for the entire site of 1,065 hectares, facilities were built on approximately half of that site, including Runway A which handles the present volume of traffic. Future plans are in preparation for the construction of Runways B and C for the purpose of further expansion of the facilities.

Narita International Airport

This sea entrance to Japan is the most representative of Japanese harbors. Here is the famous American Pier, also known as Ōsanbashi.

Numerous passenger liners and freighters pass through this harbor daily.

Port Yokohama

TOKYO

Tokyo is the largest city in the world, with its population of eleven million, and the capital of Japan. Tokyo has been the political, economic, and cultural center of Japan since 1603, when Tokugawa Ieyasu set up his shogunate in the castle town, then called Edo. At the time of the Meiji Restoration (1868), its name was changed to Tokyo, and the new emperor established it as the new imperial capital of Japan. Tokyo has been destroyed many times, by fire, earthquake, and bombing, but each time it has risen from its own ashes to become an even greater city than before. Vast construction projects, which greatly modernized the city, were carried out for the Tokyo Olympics in 1964. (See HOIKUSHA COLOR BOOKS 8 Tokyo.)

The Diet Building

Nijūbashi Bridge

The new Imperial Residence
 Here is a night view of the new imperial residence, which was completed in April 1969. The tower to the left houses lighting facilities.

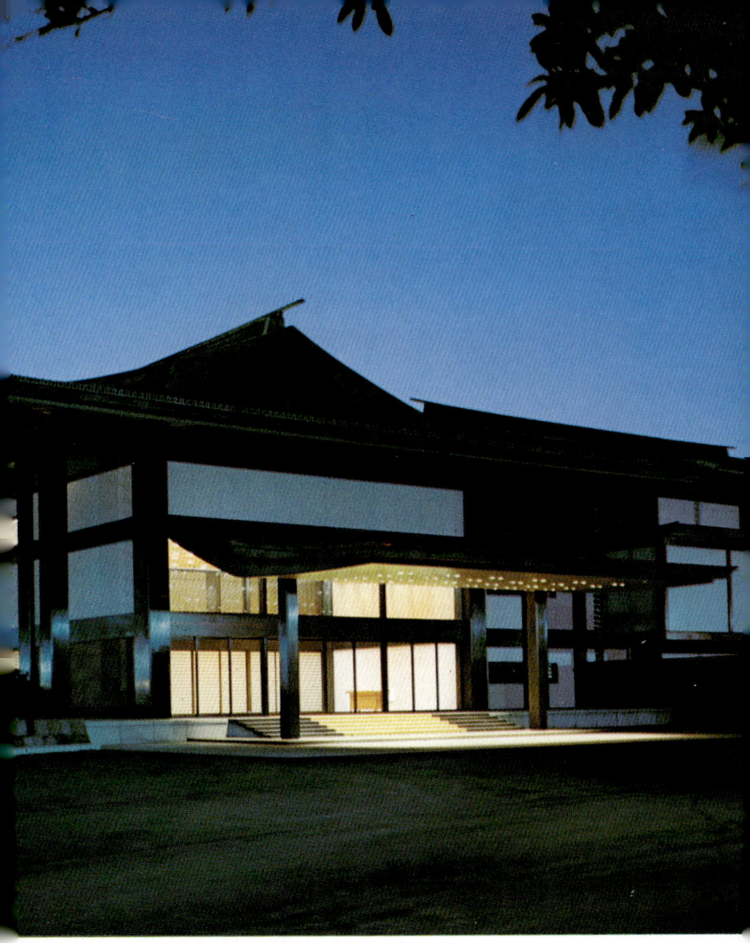

The main road to Meiji Shrine

Meiji Shrine

Meiji Shrine was built as a memorial to Emperor Meiji (1852 – 1912) and Empress Shōken (1850 – 1914). The shrine itself is surrounded by a vast park of more than 100,000 trees, which were donated by the people of Japan, creating an oasis of quiet greenery in the heart of the busy metropolis of Tokyo.

The Sports Center in Komazawa and Akasaka Mitsuke

The Sports Center consists of stadiums, gymnasiums, and other sports fields and grounds, which were built in Yoyogi and Komazawa for the 1964 Olympics in Tokyo. (above)

Akasaka and Roppongi form the new adult amusement center of Tokyo. These areas are filled with all-night restaurants, night clubs and discotheques.

Shinjuku
 Shinjuku is one of Tokyo's most modern terminal shopping centers. There are many big department stores, specialty shops, restaurants, night clubs and theaters.

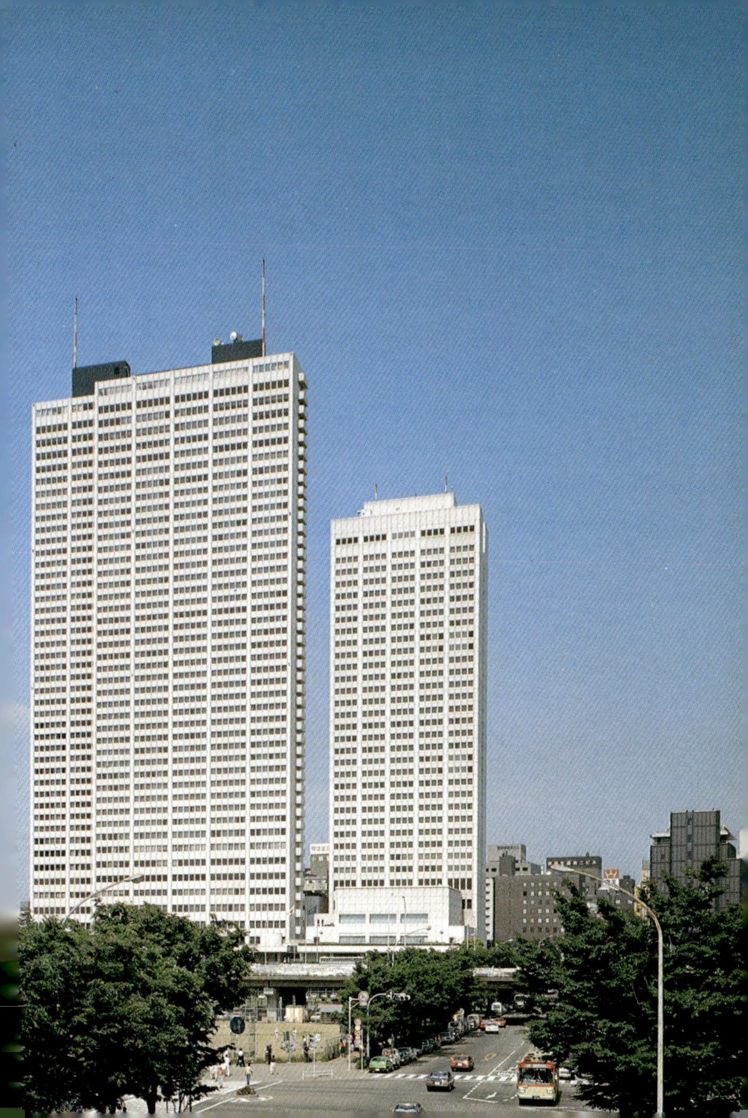

The National Museum of Western Art

Shinobazu Pond in Ueno

Ueno Park

Ueno Park is built on a hilltop, which is covered with blossoming cherry trees. Within its grounds are the National Museum, The National Museum of Science, The National Museum of Western Art, The National Museum of Modern Art, The Tokyo Municipal Art Gallery, a zoo, an aquarium, and the University of the Arts.

Asakusa area

Gate of Sensō-ji

Asakusa

Asakusa has been the people's amusement area of Tokyo for centuries. Asakusa Temple is its center, around which are shops of all descriptions. In the surrounding area are numerous theaters, movie houses, restaurants, and bars.

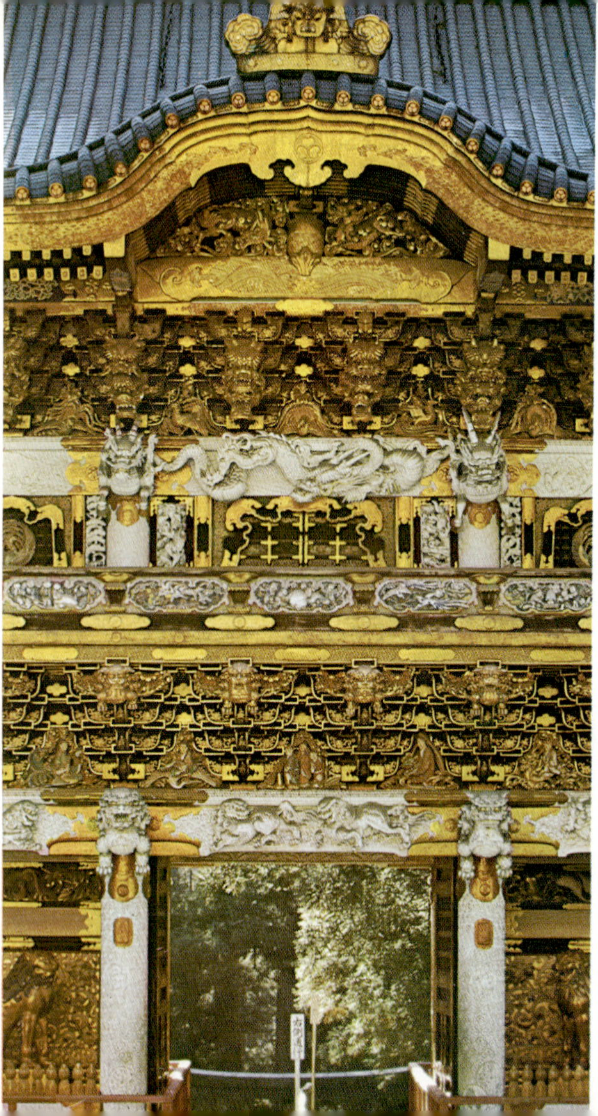

Oze Swamp and Plain —Nikkō National Park—

◀ Yōmei Gate —Nikkō—

NIKKŌ

Nikkō National Park is one of Japan's most popular sight seeing and resort areas. Nikkō is located approximately 150 kilometers north of Tokyo. It can be reached in two hours by train, or four hours by car.

The main point of interest is Tōshō Shrine, which was built in 1617, and remodelled in 1636. Within this small area is found the whole range and essence of all Japanese art. The Yōmei Gate is the most famous single work in the area.

A drive up the mountain from Tōshō Shrine of one hour and 48 hair-pin curves brings one to Kegon Falls. An elevator takes visitors to the foot of this 100 meter high and 8 meter wide waterfall. The fall completely freezes over in the winter.

Above the waterfall is Lake Chūzenji, which was formed by eruptions of the now inactive volcano, Mount Nantai. The lake lies 1,271 meters above sea level.

In the north-western part of Nikkō National Park lies Oze Swamp and Plain. This area abounds in primitive forms of plant and animal life.

Lake Chūzenji

Kegon Falls

Gate of Engaku-ji —Kamakura—

The huge bronze Buddha —Kamakura— ▶

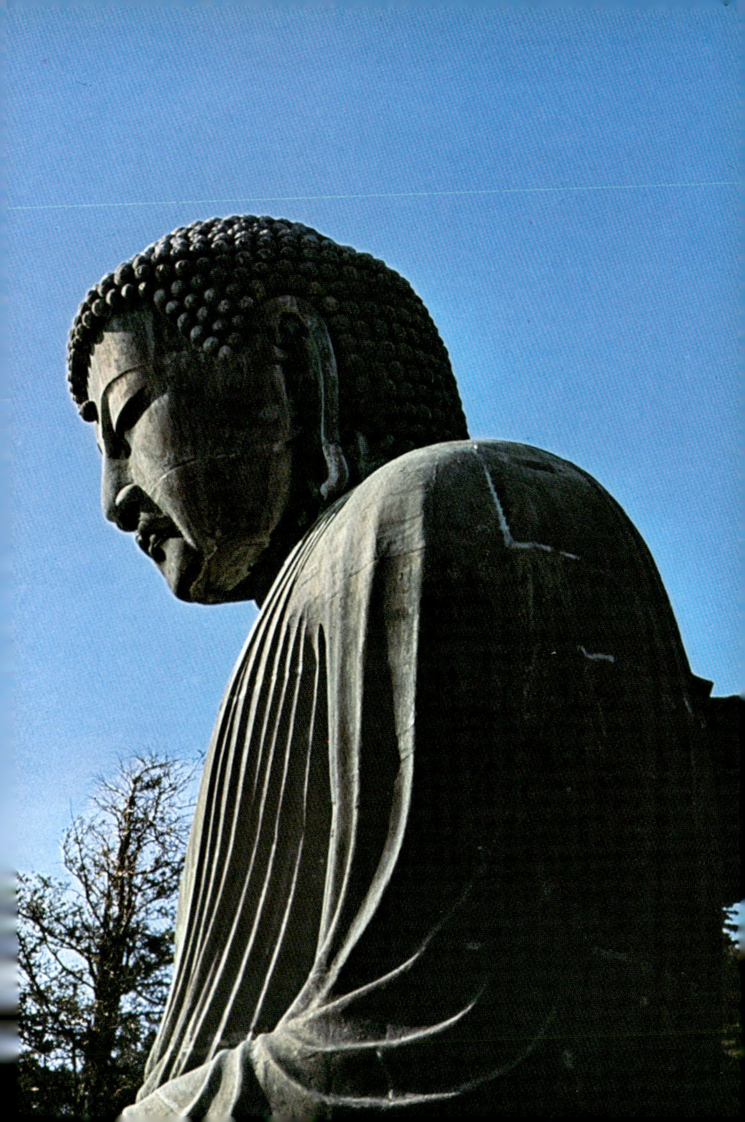

Gate of Kenchō-ji

KAMAKURA

The city of Kamakura lies at the base of the Miura Peninsula, on the shores of Sagami Bay in Kanagawa Prefecture. It can be reached by train from Tokyo in about one hour. Minamoto Yoritomo moved the center of his shogunate to Kamakura toward the end of the 12th century, and the central government remained there for the next 150 years. The city is literally filled with ancient temples and shrines, including Tsurugaoka Hachiman Shrine, the Great Buddha, and the Five Mountain Temples of Kamakura – Kenchō-ji, Engaku-ji, Jūfuku-ji, Jōchi-ji, and Jōmyō-ji. The surrounding area, with Yuigahama Swimming Area and the entertainment facilities on the island called Enoshima, combined with the historical temples and shrines mentioned above, make Kamakura a popular resort and sightseeing area for Tokyoites. Also many of its residents commute to offices in Tokyo.

Tsurugaoka Hachiman Shrine

Mount Fuji and Lake Ashi

Lake Ashi
   Lake Ashi lies in the caldera of the volcano, Mount Hakone. It is particularly famous for its reflection of Mount Fuji, commonly called "Up-side-down Fuji". It never freezes, and is popular for boating, pleasure cruising, and water skiing in the summer.

MOUNT FUJI, HAKONE, IZU

The Fuji-Hakone-Izu National Park is a huge volcanic area, which spreads throughout Kanagawa, Shizuoka, and Yamanashi Prefectures. To the north lies Mount Fuji and its five lakes; to the east Mount Hakone, Lake Ashi, and a whole string of spas and hot springs; to the south, Izu Peninsula with its mountains and beautiful beaches, and the cities of Ito and Shuzenji, which are also filled with hot springs and spas. Also convenient from Tokyo, the area serves as a year-around resort area.

Irō-zaki Point —Izu Peninsula—

Mount Fuji and Izu Sky Line

Mount Fuji

Mount Fuji rises 3,776 meters above sea level, forming Japan's highest peak. Its cone shape, surrounded by broad, flat plains, gives it a unique beauty. There are three mountain climbing paths, on which buses run up to the 1,500 meter level. In the surrounding plains area lie the Fuji Five Lakes, all famous for their beauty.

Atami City

Atami

Atami is one of Japan's favorite recreation and resort areas because of its numerous hot springs. It is located in the north-east corner of Izu Peninsula. It is the cross roads to Izu Peninsula and Hakone.

Super Express "Hikari"

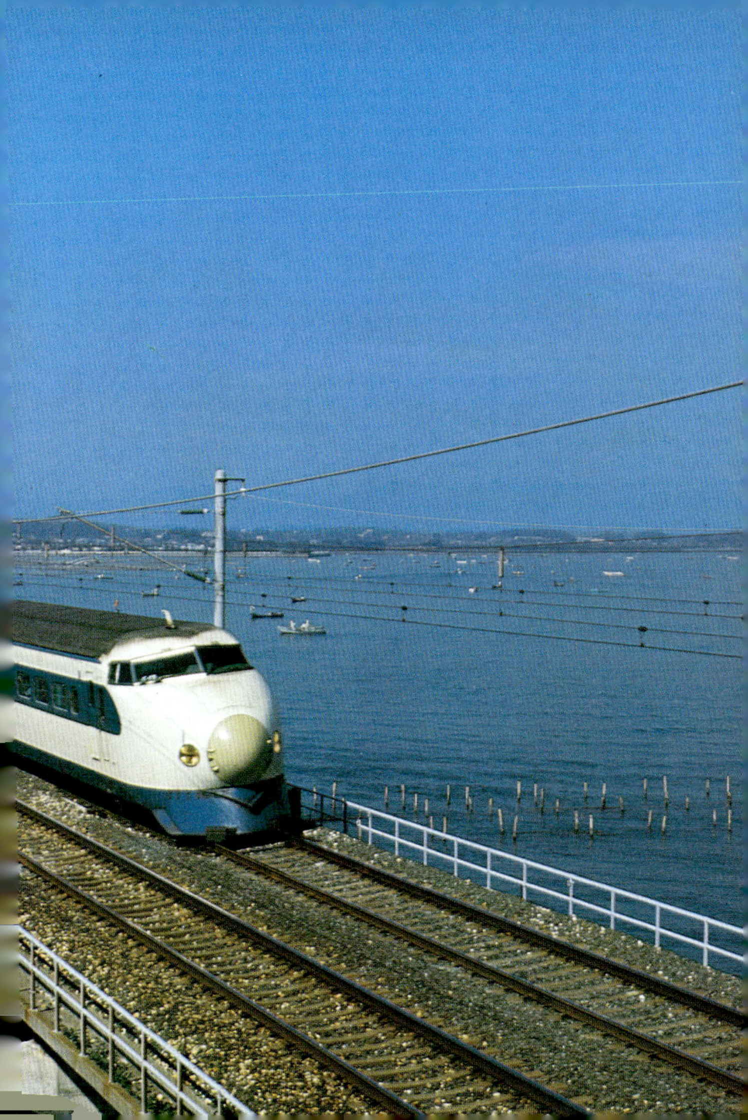

Kyoto City

KYOTO

For over 1,000 years, from 794 to 1868, Kyoto was the imperial capital of Japan. In ancient days, it was also the center of the political government, but Yoritomo moved the political center to Kamakura, and Tokugawa Ieyasu later moved it to Edo. Kyoto continued as the center of traditional culture, where Nishijin textiles and Kiyomizu pottery are produced, and such historically important sight seeing spots as Higashi Hongan-ji, Nishi Hongan-ji and Chion-in. It was not bombed during the Second World War, thus the whole city is preserved as it has been for centuries. Kyoto also is the site of many ancient festivals and rituals which are held annually. Sightseers, including foreign visitors, exceed one million per year. Kyoto can now be reached from Tokyo by train in two hours and fifty minutes on the New Tokaido Line. (See HOIKUSHA COLOR BOOKS 4 Kyoto.)

Kiyomizu-dera

Higashi Hongan-ji

Maiko – Kyoto

Cherry blossoms at Heian Shrine —Kyoto—

Kiyomizu Pottery Kiln

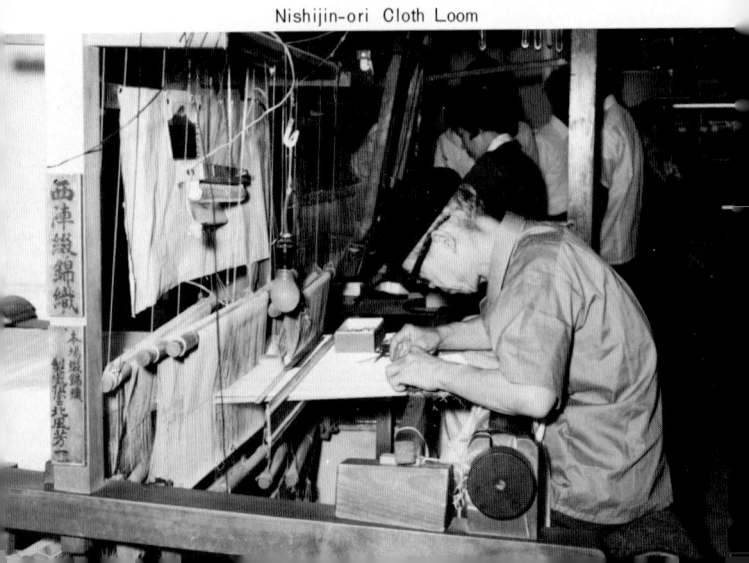

Nishijin-ori Cloth Loom

The view commanding Lake Biwa from the observatory on the top of Mt. Hiei

MOUNT HIEI and LAKE BIWA

Mount Hiei rises 848 meters above sea level, just on the boundary between Kyoto and Shiga Prefectures. Enryaku-ji, a temple which was built at the beginning of the Heian period, is located on its north-eastern side. The panoramic view from its summit is magnificent, with Kyoto to the west, Lake Biwa and the Ōmi Flatlands to the east, and Mount Ibuki to the north-east. Mount Hiei itself is covered with deep forests in which numerous varieties of wild birds flourish. Cable cars and modern highways provide pleasant transportation to the summit.

Lake Biwa, which is Japan's largest lake, is located north-east of Kyoto, in the center of Shiga Prefecture. Several islands dot its surface and the scenery around its shores is beautiful. Pleasure boats tour its surface from spring to fall.

Golden Pavilion —Kyoto—

Red leaves. ― Kyoto ―

Tōshōdai-ji

NARA

Nara was the capital of ancient Japan for 75 years, beginning in 710 A.D. The capital was moved to Kyoto in 784 A.D., and since that time, Nara has maintained its position as an important religious and sightseeing center with such important temples and shrines as Tōdai-ji, Kōfuku-ji, Yakushi-ji, Tōshōdai-ji and Kasuga Shrine. These religious edifices contain a wealth of paintings and sculpture, many of which have been designated as Important National Treasures. Many ancient festivals are held annually in Nara. The sacred deer in Nara Park add beauty and charm to the city's total atmosphere. Transportation facilities from both Osaka and Kyoto are efficient and convenient. (See HOIKUSHA COLOR BOOKS 7 Nara.)

Tōdai-ji

Yakushi-ji

Sarusawa pond and the five-storied pagoda
—Nara—

Deer —Nara Park—

Kasuga Shrine —Nara—

OSAKA

Osaka is Japan's center of commerce and industry. It was the sight of EXPO'70. It prospered as a castle town after Toyotomi Hideyoshi built his famous castle there. Since that time, it has continued to develop as the commercial capital of Japan. It is often referred to as the "Smoke Capital" because of the exhaust from its numerous industrial furnaces. It has the best private transportation system in Japan. Along with Kobe and Yokohama, Osaka is one of Japan's three main port towns. The Yodo River, with its several branches, flows through the heart of Osaka, resulting in such nicknames as the "Water Capital" and the "Capital of Bridges".

Osaka Castle

Subway

Midō-suji (The main street of Osaka)

Kansai International Airport

Nakanoshima highway —Osaka—

KŌBE

Since ancient days, Kōbe has been the center of trade with the Ryūkyū Islands and the Chinese mainland. Even today, it handles 22% of Japan's international trade. Kōbe is truly an international city, with over 35,000 people from 53 different foreign countries living within its city limits. Kōbe is surrounded by such resort areas as Suma, Maiko, Mount Rokkō, and Arima Spa.

Port Kōbe, its background is Mt. Rokkō.

Looking toward the Memorial Dome from the Memorial Cenotaph

HIROSHIMA

Hiroshima is on the coast of the Seto Inland Sea, about 340 kilometers west of Osaka. It is reached by new Sanyō line from Osaka in two hours.

The Hiroshima atom bomb was dropped on August 6, 1945. It levelled the greater part of the city in an instant and killed 200,000 people. The Atomic Bomb Memorial Dome, at the approximate epicenter of the atomic explosion, is the only structure the city has preserved in its destroyed state. Not far from the Memorial Dome is the Peace Memorial Park where the Memorial Cenotaph for the A-bomb victims stands.

Itsukushima Shrine, one of Japan's three most celebrated sights, is on the island of Miyajima west of Hiroshima. The train ride from Hiroshima to Miyajimaguchi Station takes about thirty minutes, and a 10 to 15-minute ferry boat ride from there takes you to the island.

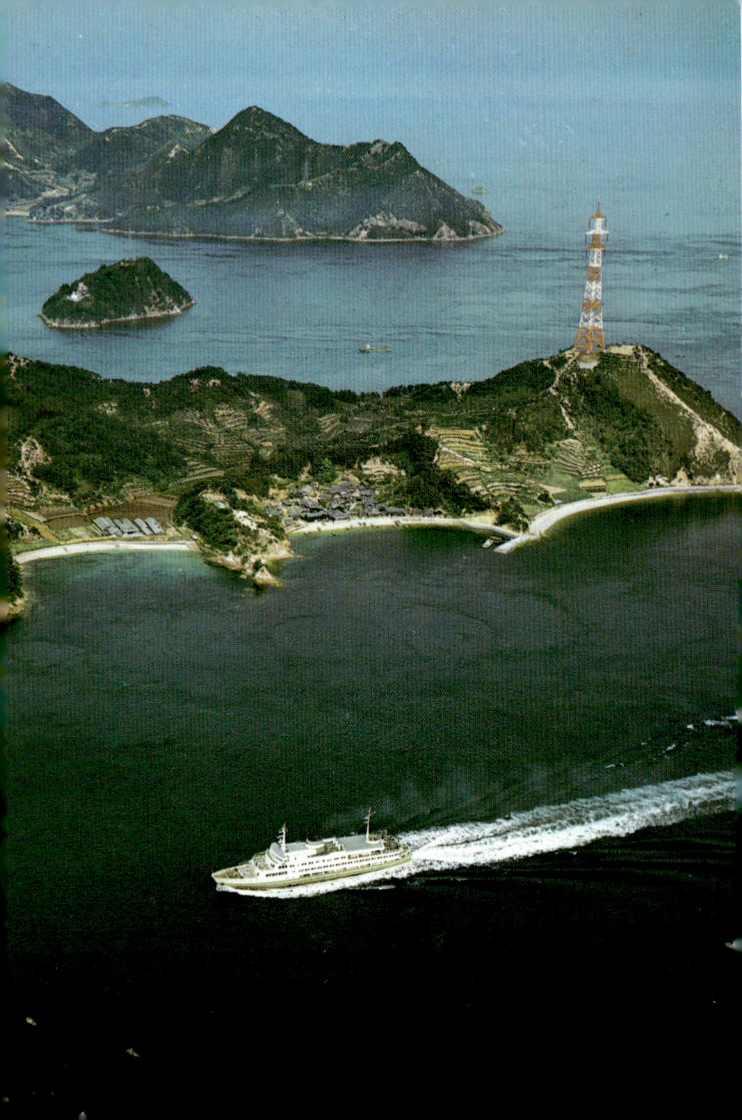

On the deck — The Seto Inland Sea —

THE SETO INLAND SEA

The Seto Inland Sea is a long narrow expanse of water surrounded by Kinki, Chūgoku, Shikoku, and Kyūshū. It is 440 kilometers long from east to west, 5 to 55 kilometers wide, and is dotted with more than 3,000 islands of various sizes. Called the "Garden of Japan", the sea and its surrounding areas have been designated as a national park. Its many recreational facilities, such as the pleasure boat connecting Osaka, Kobe, and Beppu, and the viewing platforms on the mountains along its shores provide it with brisk tourist trade the year around.

◀ The Seto Inland Sea

KYŪSHŪ

Beppu – a city of international fame for its hot springs and spas is nestled in a beautiful landscape of mountains and plateaus on the eastern shore of Kyūshū Island. The Seto Inland Sea pleasure boat line also makes a stop here.

Mount Aso is a volcano in the center of Kyūshū, famous for its large caldera – 17 kilometers east to west, and 24 kilometers north to south – said to be the largest of its kind in the world.

A well appointed bus route connects Beppu, Aso, and Kumamoto for a pleasant tour of the island.

Unzen-Amakusa National Park is located on the western shore of Kyūshū. This area is internationally famous as a sightseeing spot not only for its natural beauty, but also for the historical monuments and remains of early Japanese Christians.

Unzen Amakusa National Park

Crater of Mt. Aso

Chapel of Ōura

Nagasaki, a port city on Kyūshū's western shores, was the gateway for the introduction of Western culture and Christianity into Japan during the 16th century. Several of the old Dutch mansions have been preserved in their original state and have been designated as Important Cultural Properties. One third of the city was destroyed by the atomic bomb dropped on August 9, 1945.

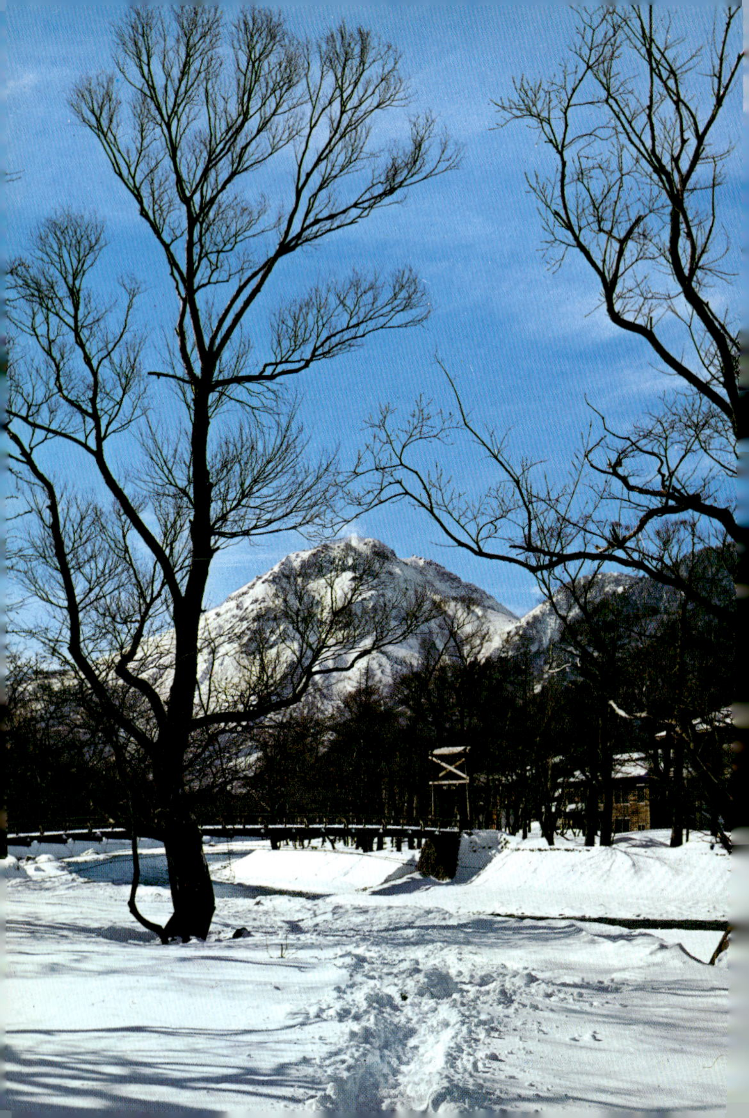

THE JAPAN ALPS

In the center of Honshū, the main island of Japan, are the Japan Alps — some peaks rise as high as 3,000 meters, and their summits are covered with snow even in midsummer. Kamikōchi is a popular mountain climbing resort area, with its hot springs, spas, cabins, and hiking trails.

◀ Kappa Bridge —Kamikōchi—

HOKKAIDŌ

Hokkaidō is the northern most island of Japan and has been developed very little because of its distance from Honshū, the main island. The average year-round temperature is 5 to 7 degrees Centigrade, and in the inland regions, drops to as low as 8 to 10 degrees Centigrade below zero in January. Forests cover 70% of its total area. A combination of warm and cold currents flowing around its shores, and its off shore areas, produce an abundance of fish of numerous varieties.

Sapporo is located in the center of its western section, and is the political, economic, and cultural center of Hokkaidō. It is an ultra-modern city which was entirely built on a plan drawn up by American city planner H. Capron. It is famous for its poplar and elm boulevards, the clock in the tower on the former Hokkaidō University campus, and the beautiful scenery in its suburbs. Sapporo was the site of the 1972 Winter Olympics.

Noboribetsu Spa is the best of its kind in Hokkaidō. It is the center of Shikotsu Toya National Park. There is an express bus between it and Sapporo. Its viewing platform affords a fine view of Hell Valley (Jigoku-dani) and Sun Swamp (Ōyu-numa).

The main street of Sapporo

Hell Valley (Jigoku-dani) in Noboribetsu

The pasture in Tsukisappu

The Snow Festival —Sapporo—

THE SNOW FESTIVAL

The Snow Festival (Yuki Matsuri) is held every February in Sapporo. During this "Festival of Beauty and Ice", historical, modern and imaginary characters are given solid form in the plaza at the central point of Sapporo's main thoroughfare.

CONTENTS

THE LAND OF JAPAN 98
By Tsuguo Murakami

An Oriental Island Country 98
Abundance of Mountains and Lack of Flatlands .. 98
Highly Varied Climate 99
Natural Disasters 100

THE FLOW OF JAPANESE CULTURE . 103
By Toshio Koma

Flourishing of the Ancient Capital
  (6th to 11th Centuries) 106
Appearance of the Warrior class
  (12th to 15th Centuries) 111
The Gun and The Cross (16th Century) 116
Japan Closes Her Doors 118
Japan Today 121

THE LAND OF JAPAN

An Oriental Island Country
The land of Japan is made up of a long narrow string of islands, the largest of which is Honshū, the central island of the group. Honshū is about the same size as Great Britain. Hokkaidō, the northern-most island, is the next in size, followed by Kyūshū and Shikoku, both to the west. Aside from these four main islands, there are numerous smaller islets especially numerous in the Seto Inland Sea, which lies between Shikoku and Honshū, and in the straits to the west of Kyūshū. Two hundred of these are inhabited. Japan is truly an island country.

The islands of Japan are spread from 24 to 45.5 degrees latitude north, and from 128 to 146 degrees longitude east. If Japan were a continent, it would, thus, be a huge country of four million square kilometers. This is the same as all the area of India and Pakistan combined. However, there is more water than land in the section of the globe covered by Japan, and the actual amount of land comes to a grand total of only 370,000 square kilometers, larger than Finland, and smaller than Morocco. This broad expanse of globe space, with comparatively little actual land, is one of the factors which has helped create the special character of Japan. Thus, within Japan are both areas cool enough to raise apples, and warm enough to raise mandarin oranges and even pineapple.

Abundance of Mountains and Lack of Flatlands
The islands of Japan are covered with a complicated network of mountains. Japan makes up one section of the circum-Pacific orogenic belt, which is part of the Great Cordillera containing the Rockies and the Andes. The Asian side of the Great Cordillera is mostly under water, and its summits form the islands of the Pacific Ocean. Japan, being part of this system, is naturally mountainous. Japan has several

mountain ranges crossing one another, which has resulted in many volcanoes. These volcanoes form the backbone of Japan's scenic beauty. Japan's National Parks are almost all centered around volcanoes or their aftereffect.

This varied mountain situation is the cause of a very rainy climate, which in turn causes twice as much erosion as in Europe. This erosion is what has built the costal plains of Japan. The geological situation here is the reason there are no vast plains stretching as far as the eye can see, like those found on the continents of America and Europe. Thus only 18% of the total land surface of Japan is tillable. On the other hand, the population of Japan exceeds one hundred million. The ratio of population to land area is 267 people to one square kilometer, a little lower than Holland, Taiwan, Belgium and China, but the ratio of population to tillable land comes to 1,647 people to one square kilometer – a much higher population rate than any other country in the world.

Highly Varied Climate

Though Japan is in the moderate climate belt, its climate is very varied, because it lies between Asia, the largest continent, and the Pacific Ocean, the largest body of water on the globe. The resulting monsoons divide Japan's annual climate changes into four seasons. Winter monsoons cause snow, monsoons cause the early summer rainy season, and the late summer typhoons. Japan's year is, thus, divided into many different clear cut poetic "moods" – cherry blossom time in April, spring greenery in May, the rainy season (*tsuyu* literally, "plum rain") in June, midsummer humid heat in July and August, the typhoon season in September and early October, chrysanthemums and autumn leaves time in late October and November, and winter snow and ice from December to February.

Natural Disasters

Japan has great natural beauty. The varied climate of Japan is the direct result of the complicated system of mountain ranges. But this situation provides not only beauty. Beautiful things have a habit of becoming frightening at times.

The volcanoes sometimes erupt, and underground activity sometimes causes highly destructive earthquakes. Great destruction is also caused by typhoons. The yearly damage is especially great in Kyūshū. It is not always the strong winds, but excess rain and abrupt changes in temperature caused by typhoons that bring about the greatest damage. However, the Japanese people refuse to be beat by this type of natural calamity and begin reconstruction immediately. Perhaps it is this training imposed by nature which made it possible for the Japanese to accomplish the almost miraculous reconstruction and progress which has been seen in Japan since the Second World War.

These are the geographical characteristics of Japan, the East Asian country that floats on the surface of the sea. The face of the land changes as the population increases. The manmade beauty of Kyoto and Nara harmonize with their natural surroundings. The beauty of Japan changes constantly to reflect the seasons of the year and the changes in the times.

Climate by Number of Days Per Month (Average from 1961 to 1990)

		Jan.	Feb.	Mar.	Apr.	May	June	July	Aug.	Sept.	Oct.	Nov.	Dec.
Sapporo	Clear	0	0	1	3	2	2	1	1	2	3	1	0
	Cloudy	13	11	12	10	11	13	15	14	9	8	10	12
	Rain	4	3	2	2	2	3	3	6	6	4	4	4
	Snow	28	25	23	6	0	—	—	—	—	1	14	25
Tokyo	Clear	9	5	4	3	2	1	1	2	1	3	6	10
	Cloudy	5	7	10	13	14	19	17	12	16	13	8	4
	Rain	2	3	5	6	6	8	5	6	8	7	4	2
	Snow	3	4	3	0	—	—	—	—	—	—	0	1
Kyoto	Clear	2	1	2	3	3	1	1	2	1	4	3	3
	Cloudy	7	8	9	11	12	16	14	9	11	9	6	5
	Rain	2	3	5	7	7	11	10	6	8	6	3	2
	Snow	11	11	6	0	—	—	—	—	—	—	0	3
Nagasaki	Clear	2	2	2	3	3	1	1	2	3	7	5	3
	Cloudy	12	11	10	12	13	17	14	8	10	7	7	11
	Rain	3	4	5	8	8	13	12	8	8	4	4	2
	Snow	7	5	1	0	—	—	—	—	—	—	0	3

Rain:Day with precipitation below 10mm is not included.

(from Rikanepyô '95)

Average Monthly Temperature (℃) (from 1961 to 1990)

	Jan.	Feb.	Mar.	Apr.	May	June	July	Aug.	Sept.	Oct.	Nov.	Dec.	Yearly
Sapporo	-4.6	-4.0	-0.1	6.4	12.0	16.1	20.2	21.7	17.2	10.8	4.3	-1.4	8.2
Tokyo	5.2	5.6	8.5	14.1	18.6	21.7	25.2	27.1	23.2	17.6	12.6	7.9	15.6
Kyoto	4.0	4.5	7.6	13.9	18.7	22.4	26.5	27.7	23.4	17.1	11.5	6.5	15.3
Nagasaki	6.4	7.0	10.1	15.2	19.0	22.3	26.6	27.6	24.3	19.0	13.7	8.8	16.7

(from Rikanenpyō '95)

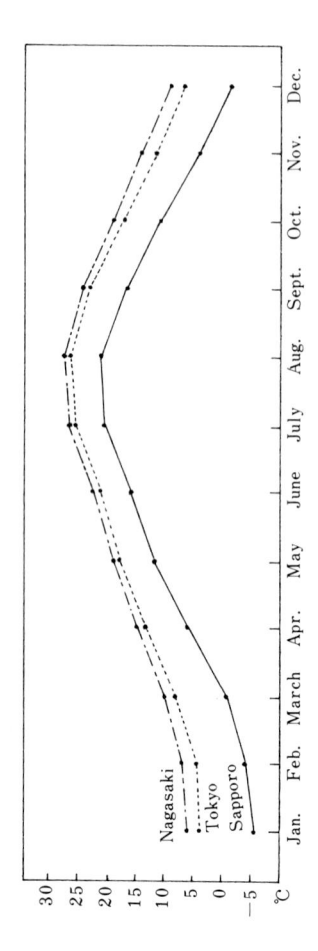

THE FLOW OF JAPANESE CULTURE

Ancient Japan

The character of a people, their culture, and the history of their country, no matter what country it may be, would be most difficult to discuss adequately in the space available here. Also, it takes more than a simple guide book for anyone to truly know and understand a people not his own, their culture, and history.

The story is told of the anthropology student who put a chimpanzee in a room to observe its habits. When the student looked through the keyhole, he found that all he could see was the curious eye of the chimpanzee staring back at him from the other side of the door. Aside from the problem of which is the monkey and which the human, we of the East and the West find ourselves today like these two living beings staring at each other through the same keyhole.

Both have deep interest in the other, have been staring for a long time, but have not yet been able to gain complete understanding of each other. In some ways, the East and the West seem farther apart than the earth and the moon.

Even among the countries of the Orient, Japan has developed in an unusual way. It seems to have been born, an entity apart, by a special dispensation of the gods. Thus one cannot say one knows Japan because one knows the Orient, and by the same token, one who knows Japan well does not necessarily have an understanding of the rest of the Orient.

As can be seen clearly by looking at a map of Japan, the four main islands of Japan form a wide curve just off the coast of the Asian mainland. The singularity of Japan is partly due to the fact that it shares no borderlines with other countries.

While England shares the same type of geographical situation, it was conquered and made a part of the Roman Empire very early in history. On the other hand, Japan was not conquered or occupied by the Mongol Empire, or any other power throughout its early history.

A peninsula of the Asian mainland protrudes out toward the center of the islands of Japan. It is the Korean Peninsula, which has acted as the pipeline between Japan and the mainland since ancient days. In other words, various aspects of culture passed through this narrow pipeline, and flowed into Japan. Japan has accepted that flow of culture, taken in what it liked, polished, assimilated, and made the foreign things its own. Thus Japan has become the treasure chest of Oriental culture. If this point is clearly understood from the start, the reader will find it easier to gain an understanding of Japan as a whole.

Japan is an extremely old country. Of course, there are much older cultures such as ancient Egypt, Mesopotamia, and ancient China, and it is true that Japan was still in the stone age at the time these other ancient cultures were flourishing.

Japan's claim to age is the length of time it has been a self-ruled single nation. Granted, the pyramids still stand along the Nile River, India's ancient temples still stand, and much of the Great China Wall still winds its way across that country, but the governments and cultures of these various countries are vastly different than they were when their monuments were built. The nation of Japan, however, has continued to rule itself and develop its culture in an unending line since around the fourth and fifth centuries.

Details as to how the nation was set up in the early days were not recorded adequately by our ancestors. All we have left are the dramatic myths of the gods giving birth to our islands, and the descendants of the sun god coming to inhabit the new land.

The more realistic officials of our neighboring country China left more factual records, which aid us in the study of our own country's history. Through these records, we find that about the third century A.D., Japan was made up of many small nations, several of which were under the rule of an empress. By means of wars and mutual agreements, the united area began to grow in size.

By the fifth century, the great Yamato Dynasty had become the strong ruler of a large territory. This territory was governed by the imperial family. The same imperial family has continued to rule Japan throughout the following centuries and down to the present. This historical fact must be understood before one can even begin to understand the people of Japan and their love for their emperor.

A Haniwa Clay Image

Flourishing of the Ancient Capital
(6th to 11th Centuries)

With its heavy natural fortress, the sea, completely surrounding it, at first glance it would seem that Japan's culture developed in a complete hothouse atmosphere. This is true, but during the long centuries of its history, Japan received strong cultural stimuli through introduction of foreign cultures three times.

The first of these was the introduction of Buddhist culture during the 6th and 7th centuries, the second was the introduction of European culture during the 16th century, and the third was the introduction of modern Western culture during the 19th century at the time of the Meiji Restoration (1868).

The third time was of especial importance because of both the extent of Western influence brought in, and to the Japanese, the high level of cultural development found in Western culture as compared to Japan at that time.

Usually when a high level culture flows suddenly into a country whose cultural level is lower, that country's own culture is overpowered and completely replaced by the new culture. However, Japan was still able to maintain its individuality under the great influx of Western culture, because of the strong national character of the Japanese people.

In 7th century Japan, there was no actual organized religion, as such. Thus Buddhism was welcomed with open arms. More than likely, the leaders of the day did not really understand the subtlety and depths of the new religion, but they were strongly attracted to the art and technology which came along with it from the mainland.

The ruling families built huge burial mounds and temples, and filled them with golden statues of Buddha with their new found knowledge.

Shotoku Taishi, a member of the imperial family, built the Hōryū-ji (P. 11) during this early period, which can still be seen today, in Ikaruga, Nara Prefecture. It is the oldest wooden structure in the world today. The statue of Buddha in its Golden Hall (P. 12) is very similar to a huge stone Buddha of the same period in China.

Seventh century Japan took up, along with the Buddhist culture, the political system of the Chinese empire. During the 8th century, a capital city called Heijōkyō was built in the

The huge bronze Buddha

northern part of Nara Prefecture. The remains of this ancient capital and articles excavated from the area can be seen at the site of the Heijōkyō palace.

The huge temples in the city of Nara were the gorgeous neck ornaments of the ancient capital. Tōshōdai-ji (P. 78) was built as a memorial to a Chinese Buddhist priest, and still stands today as it was originally built. Tōdai-ji (P. 79), built during the same period, is famous for its huge bronze Buddha, which is a symbol of the belief of the new Buddhist nation which was Japan.

The more than 16 meter tall bronze Buddha was partially destroyed in the 12th century, but it was restored to its former majesty, and is now the largest cast figure in the world, and the temple which houses it is the largest wooden structure in the world.

Toward the end of the 8th century, the government left this huge monument in Nara, and moved the capital from Heijōkyō to Kyoto, where an even larger and more beautiful city was built.

Different than Nara, Kyoto continued to prosper and maintained its position as the imperial capital until the middle of the 19th century — for more than 1,000 years.

Unfortunately, there is not much left in Kyoto from its early days as the capital. Japan's buildings have always been built of delicate wood and paper, which are easily destroyed by fire, whether they be hovels or great works of art.

Kyoto was the site of violent civil wars around the middle of the 15th century. During this period, most of the city was burned.

However, one can still see what the early government buildings were like. Heian Shrine (P. 73) was built toward the end of the 19th century according to the blueprints of the 8th century government buildings, which were found in old records. Also the Old Imperial Palace in the center of Kyoto, with its green trees and white graveled areas, still stands as it was built in the early days.

The period during which Nara (Heijōkyō) was the capital

was a time of introduction of new things from China, and the first 400 years after the capital was moved to Kyoto was a time of absorption and assimilation.

After the fall of the Tang Dynasty, China was ravaged by civil wars. Japan realized it was dangerous to send ships to China during this time, and communications with China were cut off for a very long period. Things that had come into Japan were assimilated and brought about the birth of new things which were truly Japanese.

The most epochmaking body of knowledge was the Chinese characters. The characters were simplified and the Japanese syllabary called *Kana* was born. All Chinese characters are ideographs, but the Japanese syllabary developed from them are a sort of alphabet, in which the characters represent only sounds. Women were taught to read and write *kana*, and during the first part of the 11th century, a court lady named Murasaki Shikibu wrote the first full length novel in the world — the 54 volumes *The Tale of Genji* (Genji Monogatari).

The Old Imperial Palace

Later, drawings were added, and the famous *Tale of Genji Scroll* (Genji Monogatari Emaki: P. 16) was created. The novel and the pictures were written and drawn on long scrolls. The drawings give a good idea of various aspects of court life of the time.

By this time, Buddhism was widely practiced even among the common people. Wealthy aristocrats built villas and temples in Kyoto and the surrounding area, which are still standing and can be seen today. The Phoenix Hall of the Byōdō-in in the southern suburbs is a good example of these gorgeous temples. The building, which is shaped like a huge bird with outstretched wings, seems as though it might fly off to the heavens at any instant. It aptly expresses the desire for eternal life held by Fujiwara Yorimichi, the powerful lord who built it. Yorimichi built this temple and the huge golden Amida Buddha statue inside, as a prayer for guidance to the pure world where the Buddha lives.

One can easily notice a marked difference between this Buddha and the Buddha of Hōryū-ji in Nara, which was mentioned earlier. The difference between these two statues shows the progress and the Japanization of Buddhism brought about from the Nara to the Heian period, and is the key to the secret of a true understanding of Japanese culture.

The Phoenix Hall of the Byōdō-in

Appearance of the Warrior Class
(12th to 15th Centuries)

While the aristocrats were building temples and discussing literary and artistic problems in the capital Kyoto, a large change was taking place in the agricultural area of the eastern part of Japan. The new warrior class was beginning to rise and make its power felt.

At first these warriors were the overseers of the outlying manors owned by the aristocrats, but these overseers began to exercise power on their own. They began to unite among themselves. They built up a large store of weapons, and formed battle groups. Finally large clans were formed. The strongest and highest class of the clans were the Genji and the Heike clans.

Toward the middle of the 12th century, the aristocrats decided to use the strength of these clans in their struggle for power. The aristocrats, who used force by means of the clans, were highly criticised by the conservative aristocrats. The aristocrats did not realize what they had done till they found that the real power of government was rapidly being taken over by the warriors. For the physically and militarily stronger country warriors, the seizing of power from the aristocrats was like taking candy from a baby.

Part of the long picture scroll entitled *The Heiji Chronicle Picture Scroll* (Heiji Monogatari Emaki), which tells of these battles is owned by the Boston Art Museum. It clearly depicts the dress and manner of the warriors of the day, just as they were coming into power.

The Heike grasped the power of the government first, but they were finally defeated and lost the reigns of the government to the Genji clan. Minamoto Yoritomo, leader of the Genji clan, moved his political capital away from Kyoto where the aristocrats still were powerful, to Kamakura. There Yoritomo built the impressive Tsurugaoka Hachiman Shrine (P. 63). Genji warriors were all firm believers in the god Hachiman.

The Heiji Chronicle Picture Scroll

Kamakura was suddenly transformed from a quiet fishing village to the very center of life in Japan. It must be remembered that Yoritomo's political power had been entrusted to him by the emperor himself, who still resided in Kyoto. Throughout the history of Japan, and all its changes and shifts in power, no warrior ever tried to become the absolute sovereign ruler of the country.

The warrior class began to create a culture of their own. But outside of horsemanship and the art of the bow and arrow, the aristocrats still far outshone the countrified warriors in cultural accomplishments. The warriors produced violent, realistic paintings and sculpture, but little that had really been created by them as a class.

Zen was introduced into Japan about this time. The Mongol hordes began to spread their power throughout the Asian continent, and Zen priests of the Sung Dynasty in China escaped to Japan in large numbers.

It was only natural that the Zen they preached struck sympathetic chords in the hearts of the warriors of Japan. Zen demands that one discover one's true self and become one with eternal truth. It is not a matter of praying to anyone or anything. One depends only on one's own strength in the process of attaining enlightenment. Warriors, who daily faced death on the battlefields, were strongly attracted to this new religion.

Kenchō-ji (P. 62) in Kamakura was built around the middle of the 13th century. It is the largest and most important of the Five Great Zen Temples of Kamakura.

It is strange to me that there has been so much written on the subject of Zen. Zen only has reality or meaning in actual practice, and the searching of the self for the gaining of enlightenment. The process and its result are different for each person – it is a very individual religion. It is useless to explain such a religion, and the more it is explained, the less is understood about it.

In Kyoto is the famous garden made only of rocks and pebbles called Ryōan-ji (P. 4). It is also a Zen temple. Tourists flock to this garden daily and study its stones with deeply furrowed brows. When you join them don't be discouraged, none of them understand any more or less about its meaning than you do. If you feel you have gained some sort of feeling or insight from the atmosphere of this garden, you will probably be on the right track toward an understanding of "things Japanese."

Let us return once more to Kamakura. The storm of the Mongol hordes, which had already devastated two continents, finally made its way to Japan. Japan was lucky to have her government in the hands of highly trained warriors, and the Mongols were unlucky because of the fact that they knew absolutely nothing of the geography of Japan.

The Mongols tried twice to invade the northern shores of Kyūshū, but both times they were met by violent typhoons which destroyed their ships and drove them back to the mainland. Kublai Khan was not able to conquer Japan, and

Zen Priests Meditating

Japan was never included in his great empire. This is a matter of great pride even to the Japanese people of the present day.

During the 14th century, there was once more a shift in power in Japan. The aristocrats rose up to take revenge against the warrior class, and there was a long period of civil wars. Finally, the Ashikagas gained power and set up a new government in Kyoto.

The Golden Pavilion (Kinkaku-ji: P. 76) was built in Kyoto as a symbol of the power of the new government. The original building was burned down by a young priest who was jealous of its beauty. It was immediately rebuilt, and stands today in glorious golden beauty. The sun reflecting off its golden walls takes the viewer back to the atmosphere of the late 14th century.

Toward the middle of the 15th century, the Ashikaga family began to lose its power and the small daimyo in the outlying territories rapidly seized the reigns of the government. Problems of governmental control arose, and once again civil war broke out.

This war divided the country into two large armies, and Kyoto, the main battle area, suffered heavy damage. This series of battles is called the Ōnin Rebellion by historians. This is a name to be remembered, because the two world famous traditional Japanese arts – Ikebana and Tea Ceremony – have important ties with this rebellion.

The head of the Ashikaga shogunate at the time of the Ōnin Rebellion was Ashikaga Yoshimasa. Yoshimasa had no talent or interest in the affairs of government, but he had a great sense of the artistic and was an important patron of the arts. He became bored and disappointed with his tedious life as government administrator, so he built himself a beautiful villa in the eastern outskirts of Kyoto, where he retired to spend his life enjoying beautiful things and creating new art.

He had a *tokonoma* (alcove) made in his villa, at the foot of Mount Higashiyama, in which he displayed paintings and other art objects. He also arranged flowers (P. 20) to add natural beauty to the display. Tea had been introduced into Japan at a much earlier date, but it was Yoshimasa who began the practice of drinking tea while viewing and discussing art objects and the beauties of nature.

The Tea Ceremony (P. 24) was canonized 100 years later, as an art of physical and mental formality and discipline, by Sen no Rikyū. But it was Yoshimasa who actually first brought the drinking of tea to the level of an art.

The art of Noh drama also began its growth, as the art we know today, during this period. The artistic and social level of Noh was raised by the patronage of Yoshimitsu, Yoshimasa's grandfather, and through the writings and activities of the actor Zeami, the perfector of the art (P. 29).

Three of the living traditional arts of Japan today – Noh, Ikebana, and Tea Ceremony – were all born about the same time. These have been recognized the world over as great arts, not for their exoticism, but because they have a universality in their silences and movements, which brings the viewer, as well as the artist, to a deeper understanding of the self and the universe in which he lives, and enriches his life.

The Gun and The Cross
(16th Century)

The civil wars had brought all Japan to a state of complete chaos by the 16th century. The Ashikaga shoguns had lost all the power they ever had, and the country daimyo were becoming stronger and stronger. The daimyo spent their days in protecting their own territories and fighting to take that of their neighbors.

This was the situation in Japan when the second great influx of foreign culture came about.

In 1549, a single European landed at Kagoshima in Kyūshū. He was a Spanish missionary. He brought along with him a culture which was entirely new to the people of Japan. He only spent two years in Japan, but he firmly planted the Christian gospel in the Oriental wasteland that was Japan.

This Spanish missionary was not, however, the first European to visit Japanese soil. A few years earlier, a Portugese ship had landed on the shores of a small island south of Kyūshū. Their contribution to Japan was the gun. Thus before the Christian God was able to make his way into Japan, the devil had gotten his tools of destruction introduced. Perhaps, after all, this is only natural, since without evil, there is no need for God.

Christianity was welcomed, but the gun was welcomed on a much larger scale and with much greater enthusiasm. Only thirty years later Japanese-made guns were being used in large numbers on her own battlefields.

After the first Spanish missionary, the church sent a constant stream of missionaries to continue his work. Most of the foreign ships after this time landed at Hirado and Nagasaki (P. 91), resulting in a most exotic atmosphere in these two ports.

The daimyo supported the missionaries because the missionaries threatened to change the landing point of foreign vessels to further south in Kyūshū if support for their cause was refused. Thus, Christianity flourished because the feudal lords wanted the trade and subsequent prosperity that came along with it. As a result, churches, colleges, and seminaries were built here and there throughout the country.

The reunification of Japan began to come about at great speed, and along with the amalgamation of political power, the church also gained power. However, before long, it became clear to the military leaders that the teachings of Christianity were in direct opposition to the warrior code – Christianity taught loyalty to God, and that man must not kill his fellow human beings, whereas it was necessary in the military government for the warriors to be loyal to their feudal lords and to kill others to gain power for him.

Persecution of Christians began with crucifixions and all other types of brutality imaginable. After the last desperate resistance on the Shimabara Peninsula, Christianity was completely wiped out.

The last twenty or thirty years of the 16th century, after all the battles were fought and Japan was united, were golden years of peace. Those who had survived the wars basked in the sheer joy of living. They welcomed new culture from Europe and a few Japanese even made trips abroad. Some historians refer to this period of human freedom as the "Japanese Renaissance".

Japan Closes Her Doors

At the beginning of the 17th century, Tokugawa Ieyasu set up the Edo Shogunate, and Japan became a stronger country than it had ever been before. As Minamoto Yoritomo had done many years before, Ieyasu also moved his government from aristocratic Kyoto, this time to the castle town Edo, in the east of Japan. This was the birth of the present capital of Japan, Tokyo.

Ieyasu portioned out the land to his retainers, and let them each rule their own fief. These feudal lords built strong fortresslike castles, around which they gathered artisans and merchants to form castle towns.

At present, many cities throughout Japan that were built in this way as castle towns still exist as modern cities. Most of the castles were destroyed around the time of the Meiji Restoration, but their walls and moats still remain as reminders of their past glory.

Himeji Castle (P. 9) is one of the best examples of the beauty and size of these edifices. It is also known as the "White Heron Castle".

The Tokugawa shogunate, with Edo as its capital, ruled all of Japan for over two centuries and a half. It was able to accomplish this feat by strictly controlling not only the political and economic aspects of the country, but the very thoughts and details of the personal life of the people of Japan. Religion was, of course, no exception, and not overlooked. Christianity was considered a menace and a direct threat to the government. Thus both Christianity and the foreign trade that had come along with it were absolutely prohibited. Travel by Japanese citizens outside of the country, as well as entry into the country by all foreigners except the Dutch, was strictly prohibited. The Dutch were only allowed on the manmade islands called Dejima in Nagasaki harbor, and even landing on this island was allowed only if the Hollanders in question swore not to attempt to spread or preach any type of religion.

In this way, Japan completely closed her gates to the

Western world and her four islands became shrouded in a mystic, unpenetrable veil. Many historians point to the strict closed-door policies of the Tokugawa era as the cause of Japan's lack of cultural modernization and progress, which is still in evidence to a great extent even today.

However, the strict system provided for great internal peace and security. Industry and transportation showed great progress, and the economic level was high. And the merchant class rose to a position of leadership in the society.

The warrior class considered the merchants, who were always concerned with money matters, far below consideration as even human beings. The Tokugawa shogunate, even from the beginning, had placed the merchant class lowest on the social ladder — the order was warrior, farmer, artisan, and merchant. But the merchants did not let this classification keep them down, because they were well aware that during a period of peace, money is much stronger than social position.

Osaka became the center of economic activity for the whole country, and is known to this day as a town of merchants. Toyotomi Hideyoshi brought about the birth of Osaka when he built Osaka Castle (P. 82), and it was from the time Hideyoshi ruled the country that merchants gathered and set up business outside the walls of his gorgeous castle.

It was these merchants who gathered products and materials from all over the country to be used for the construction and establishment of the new Tokugawa capital Edo. And it goes without saying that they gained great profit from this project.

Bunraku (P. 29) is the theatrical art which developed under the loyal patronage of the merchants of Osaka. This combination of puppets, *Shamisen* and jōruri narration, expressed in its dramas the human sadness and loneliness, and their struggle to maintain their individual integrity under the strict feudalistic system.

During the 18th century, development of the Kanto Plains area brought the population of Edo to one million — giving it full status as a metropolis. With the shogun's castle as its

Eisen / Summer style attire

center, and the daimyo from the outlying districts being required to spend most of their time in attendance on the shogun, over 50% of the population of Edo was of the warrior class, making it truly a military capital. However, merchants were also numerous and prosperous in the new capital.

The Kanda Festival is held in the summer, and was enthusiastically participated in by the townspeople of Edo, as it is by the townspeople of Tokyo today. The straight forward, rough and tumble spirit of the people of Edo brought about the birth of an entirely different cultural atmosphere than that of Osaka.

Kabuki (P. 28), which began to appear first around the beginning of the 17th century, reached its zenith as the gorgeous stage art we know today, toward the middle of the 18th century. The remarkable spread of the popularity of the *ukiyo-e* woodblock print came about around the same time, and the names Utamaro and Kiyonaga became almost household words among the townspeople all over Japan.

Western world and her four islands became shrouded in a mystic, unpenetrable veil. Many historians point to the strict closed-door policies of the Tokugawa era as the cause of Japan's lack of cultural modernization and progress, which is still in evidence to a great extent even today.

However, the strict system provided for great internal peace and security. Industry and transportation showed great progress, and the economic level was high. And the merchant class rose to a position of leadership in the society.

The warrior class considered the merchants, who were always concerned with money matters, far below consideration as even human beings. The Tokugawa shogunate, even from the beginning, had placed the merchant class lowest on the social ladder — the order was warrior, farmer, artisan, and merchant. But the merchants did not let this classification keep them down, because they were well aware that during a period of peace, money is much stronger than social position.

Osaka became the center of economic activity for the whole country, and is known to this day as a town of merchants. Toyotomi Hideyoshi brought about the birth of Osaka when he built Osaka Castle (P. 82), and it was from the time Hideyoshi ruled the country that merchants gathered and set up business outside the walls of his gorgeous castle.

It was these merchants who gathered products and materials from all over the country to be used for the construction and establishment of the new Tokugawa capital Edo. And it goes without saying that they gained great profit from this project.

Bunraku (P. 29) is the theatrical art which developed under the loyal patronage of the merchants of Osaka. This combination of puppets, *Shamisen* and jōruri narration, expressed in its dramas the human sadness and loneliness, and their struggle to maintain their individual integrity under the strict feudalistic system.

During the 18th century, development of the Kanto Plains area brought the population of Edo to one million — giving it full status as a metropolis. With the shogun's castle as its

Eisen / Summer style attire

center, and the daimyo from the outlying districts being required to spend most of their time in attendance on the shogun, over 50% of the population of Edo was of the warrior class, making it truly a military capital. However, merchants were also numerous and prosperous in the new capital.

The Kanda Festival is held in the summer, and was enthusiastically participated in by the townspeople of Edo, as it is by the townspeople of Tokyo today. The straight forward, rough and tumble spirit of the people of Edo brought about the birth of an entirely different cultural atmosphere than that of Osaka.

Kabuki (P. 28), which began to appear first around the beginning of the 17th century, reached its zenith as the gorgeous stage art we know today, toward the middle of the 18th century. The remarkable spread of the popularity of the *ukiyo-e* woodblock print came about around the same time, and the names Utamaro and Kiyonaga became almost household words among the townspeople all over Japan.

Japan Today

The recent history of Japan has become a part of modern world history, and is thus fairly well-known.

In 1853, Commodore Perry, with his four ships, landed in Japan, and forced the abolition of the long standing isolation policy of Japan. From the standpoint of the world situation, it was necessary for Japan to adopt an open door policy at this time, but internal political problems caused many complicated problems for the government and the people of Japan over this revolutionary step.

The Edo shogunate was thrown out of power, and the emperor once more took over the reins of the government and immediately set out toward the swift modernization of all aspects of Japanese life. This third and most violent influx of foreign culture completely inundated Japan with its force and vigor.

The Ship-building industry

The renovations introduced in this movement toward "civilization and enlightenment" changed the lives of the people of Japan from the very roots. There were, of course, contradictions in the new life alongside traditional arts and values. The Japanese suffered great agonies in their attempts to find harmony between the old and the new. The present culture of Japan is the result of these attempts to assimilate and harmonize.

The life of the present-day citizen of Tokyo, the largest city in the world, may in many ways seem more Western than in Western cities. It is sometimes difficult for even the Japanese themselves to find anything left of the old culture in their busy lives. But if one looks closely, one will find that underneath the surface, the old traditions and values, that were developed over a period of two thousand years, are still very much alive and a strong force in the basic daily lives of the people of Japan.

I sincerely hope that what I have written here will be of some small help as a guide to the discovery of the truly Japanese aspects of life in modern Japan. As I write this, the wind is whispering through the pine trees, and the birds are singing in their branches on the hill outside my window. Japanese beauty is still all around us in the natural, simple beauty of our land.

Tokyo
- Tokyo Prince Hotel — Tel. (03)3432-1111
- Tokyo Station Hotel — Tel. (03)3231-2511
- Yamanoue Hotel — Tel. (03)3293-2311

Yokohama
- Hotel Empire — Tel. (045)851-1431
- Hotel New Grand — Tel. (045)681-1841
- The Hotel Yokohama — Tel. (045)662-1321
- Yokohama Tokyu Hotel — Tel. (045)311-1682

Kyoto
- Biwako Hotel — Tel. (0775)24-1255
- Hotel Fujita Kyoto — Tel. (075)222-1511
- Hotel Lake Biwa — Tel. (0775)85-2511
- Hotel New Kyoto — Tel. (075)801-2111
- Hotel Sunflower Kyoto — Tel. (075)761-9111
- Hotel The Mount Hiei — Tel. (075)701-2111
- Kyoto Grand Hotel — Tel. (075)341-2311
- Kyoto Hotel — Tel. (075)211-5111
- Kyoto International Hotel — Tel. (075)222-1111
- Kyoto Palaceside Hotel — Tel. (075)431-8171
- Kyoto Park Hotel — Tel. (075)525-3111
- Kyoto Royal Hotel — Tel. (075)223-1234
- Kyoto Tokyu Hotel — Tel. (075)341-2411
- Kyoto Tower Hotel — Tel. (075)361-3211
- Miyako Hotel — Tel. (075)771-7111
- New Miyako Hotel — Tel. (075)661-7111

Osaka

Hotel Echo Osaka	Tel. (06)633-1141
Hotel Hanshin	Tel. (06)344-1661
Hotel Nikko Osaka	Tel. (06)244-1111
Hotel Plaza	Tel. (06)453-1111
New Hankyu Hotel	Tel. (06)372-5101
Osaka Castle Hotel	Tel. (06)942-2401
Osaka Daiichi Hotel	Tel. (06)341-4411
Osaka Grand Hotel	Tel. (06)202-1212
Osaka International Hotel	Tel. (06)941-2661
Tennoji Miyako Hotel	Tel. (06)779-1501
Osaka Royal Hotel	Tel. (06)448-1121
Osaka Tokyu Hotel	Tel. (06)373-2411
Toyo Hotel	Tel. (06)372-8181

Kobe

Kobe Portopia Hotel	Tel. (078)302-1111
Sannomiya Terminal Hotel	Tel. (078)291-0001
Oriental Hotel	Tel. (078)331-8111
Rokko Oriental Hotel	Tel. (078)891-0333
Rokkosan Hotel	Tel. (078)891-0301
Takarazuka Hotel	Tel. (0797)87-1151

Nara

Nara Hotel	Tel. (0742)26-3300
Nara Royal Hotel	Tel. (0742)34-1131

HOIKUSHA COLOR BOOKS
ENGLISH EDITIONS

Book Size 4″×6″

① KATSURA
② TOKAIDO Hiroshige
③ EMAKI
④ KYOTO
⑤ UKIYOE
⑥ GEM STONES
⑦ NARA
⑨ KYOTO GARDENS
⑩ IKEBANA
⑫ JAPANESE CASTLES
⑮ N O H
⑯ HAWAII
⑰ JAPAN
⑱ BUDDHIST IMAGES
⑲ OSAKA
⑳ HOKUSAI
㉑ ORIGAMI
㉒ JAPANESE SWORDS
㉓ GOLDFISH
㉔ SUMI-E
㉕ SHELLS OF JAPAN
㉖ FOLK ART
㉗ TOKYO NIKKO FUJI
㉘ NATIONAL FLAGS
㉙ BONSAI
㉚ UTAMARO
㉛ TEA CEREMONY
㉜ PAPER DOLLS
㉝ JAPANESE CERAMICS
㉞ MODEL CARS
㉟ CREATIVE ORIGAMI
㊱ Z E N
㊲ KIMONO
㊳ CHINESE COOKING
㊴ KYOGEN
㊵ NOH MASKS
㊶ LIVING ORIGAMI
㊸ OSAKA CASTLE
㊹ BUNRAKU
㊺ TOKYO SUBWAYS
㊻ GIFT WRAPPING
㊼ SHINKANSEN

COLORED ILLUSTRATIONS FOR NATURALISTS

Text in Japanese, with index in Lation or English.

Book Size 6″ × 8″

- BUTTERFLIES of JAPAN
- INSECTS of JAPAN vol.1
- INSECTS of JAPAN vol.2
- SHELLS of JAPAN vol.1
- BIRDS of JAPAN
- ROCKS
- ECONOMIC MINERALS
- HERBACEOUS PLANTS of JAPAN vol.1
- HERBACEOUS PLANTS of JAPAN vol.2
- HERBACEOUS PLANTS of JAPAN vol.3
- SEAWEEDS of JAPAN
- TREES and SHRUBS of JAPAN
- MOTHS of JAPAN vol.1
- MOTHS of JAPAN vol.2
- SHELLS of JAPAN vol.2
- FRUITS
- ECONOMIC MINERALS vol.2
- FRESHWATER FISHES of JAPAN
- GARDEN PLANTS of the WORLD vol.1
- GARDEN PLANTS of the WORLD vol.2
- GARDEN PLANTS of the WORLD vol.3
- GARDEN PLANTS of the WORLD vol.4
- GARDEN PLANTS of the WORLD vol.5
- THE FRESHWATER PLANKTON of JAPAN
- MEDICINAL PLANTS of JAPAN
- VEGETABLE CROPS of JAPAN
- SHELLS of the WORD vol.1
- SHELLS of the WORD vol.2
- THE MARINE PLANKTON of JAPAN
- EARLY STAGES of JAPANESE MOTHS vol.1
- EARLY STAGES of JAPANESE MOTHS vol.2
- FOSSILS
- WOODY PLANTS of JAPAN vol.1
- WOODY PLANTS of JAPAN vol.2
- BRYOPHYTES of JAPAN

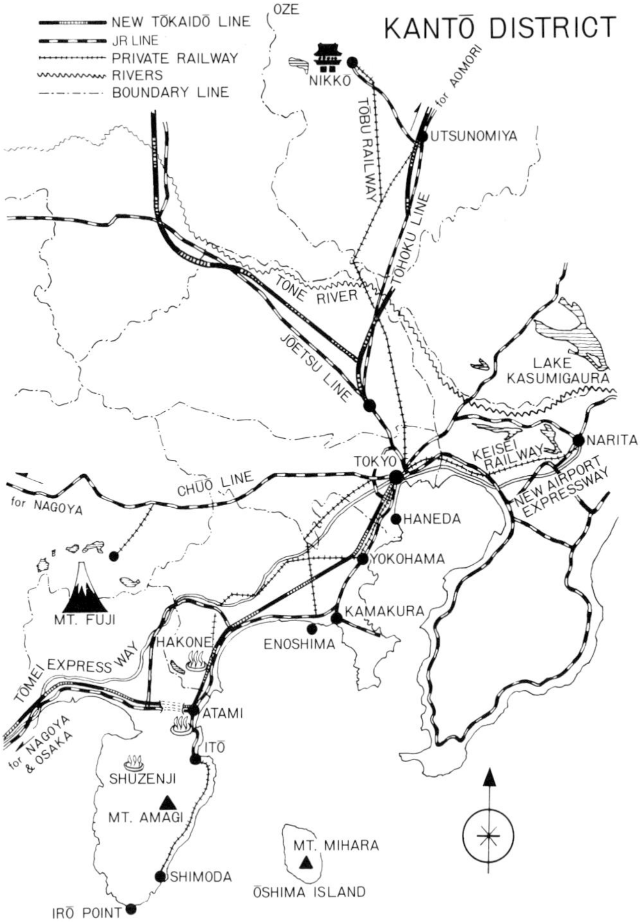
KANTŌ DISTRICT
NEW TŌKAIDŌ LINE
JR LINE
PRIVATE RAILWAY
RIVERS
BOUNDARY LINE
OZE
NIKKŌ
for AOMORI
TŌBU RAILWAY
UTSUNOMIYA
TOHOKU LINE
TONE RIVER
JŌETSU LINE
LAKE KASUMIGAURA
NARITA
KEISEI RAILWAY
NEW AIRPORT EXPRESSWAY
TOKYO
CHŪŌ LINE
for NAGOYA
HANEDA
YOKOHAMA
MT. FUJI
KAMAKURA
ENOSHIMA
HAKONE
TŌMEI EXPRESS WAY
ATAMI
for NAGOYA & OSAKA
ITŌ
SHUZENJI
MT. AMAGI
MT. MIHARA
ŌSHIMA ISLAND
SHIMODA
IRŌ POINT

KINKI DISTRICT

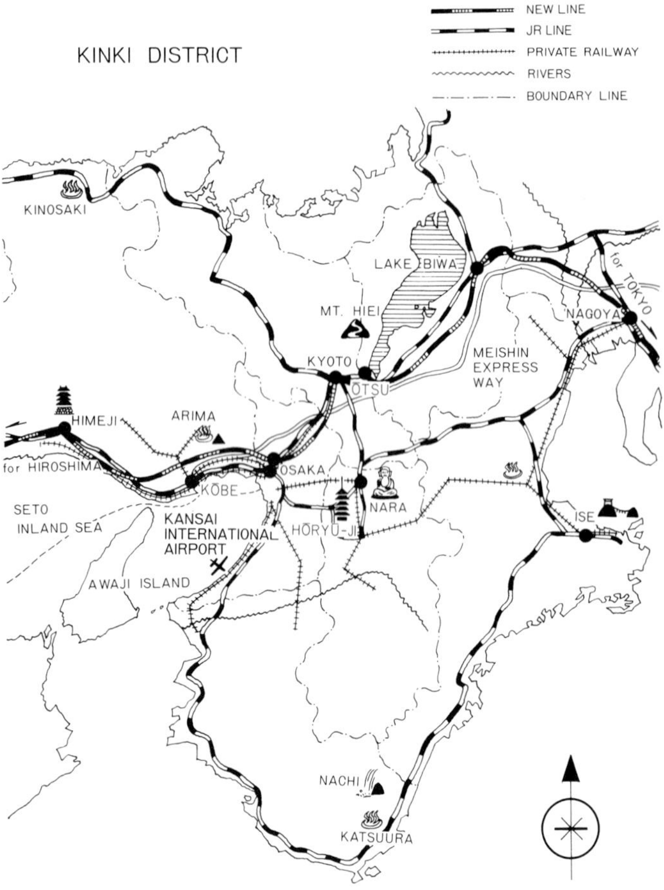

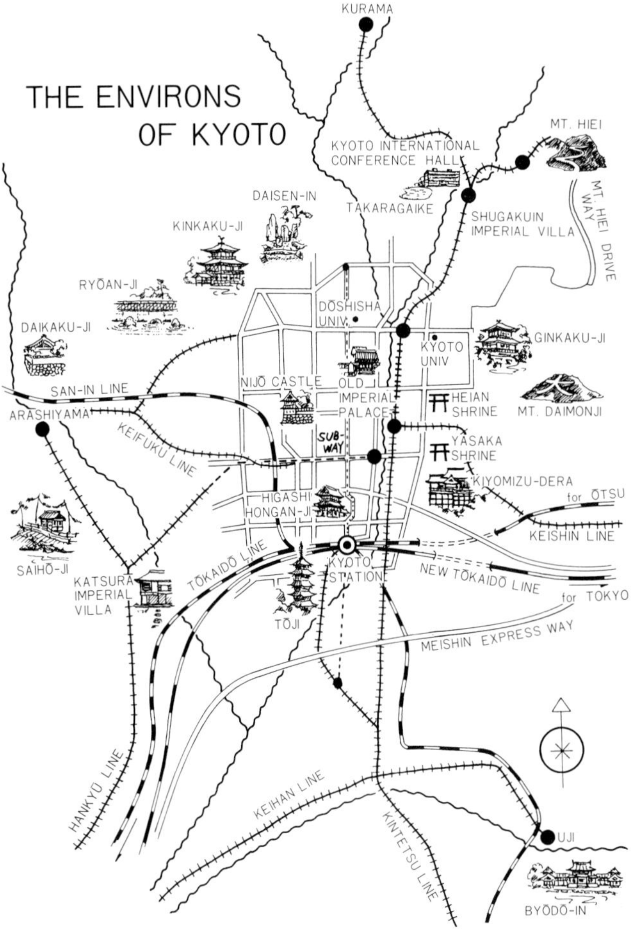
THE ENVIRONS
OF KYOTO
KURAMA
MT. HIEI
KYOTO INTERNATIONAL
CONFERENCE HALL
TAKARAGAIKE
SHUGAKUIN
IMPERIAL VILLA
MT. HIEI WAY
MT. HIEI DRIVE
DAISEN-IN
KINKAKU-JI
RYŌAN-JI
DAIKAKU-JI
DŌSHISHA
UNIV.
KYOTO
UNIV
GINKAKU-JI
NIJŌ CASTLE
OLD
IMPERIAL
PALACE
HEIAN
SHRINE
MT. DAIMONJI
SAN-IN LINE
ARASHIYAMA
KEIFUKU LINE
SUB-
WAY
YASAKA
SHRINE
KIYOMIZU-DERA
for ŌTSU
HIGASHI
HONGAN-JI
KEISHIN LINE
TŌKAIDŌ LINE
KYOTO
STATION
NEW TŌKAIDŌ LINE
SAIHŌ-JI
KATSURA
IMPERIAL
VILLA
for TOKYO
TŌJI
MEISHIN EXPRESS WAY
HANKYŪ LINE
KEIHAN LINE
KINTETSU LINE
UJI
BYŌDŌ-IN

Hotels in Japan

Tokyo

Akasaka Prince Hotel	Tel. (03)3234-1111
Akasaka Tokyu Hotel	Tel. (03)3580-2311
Fairmont Hotel	Tel. (03)3262-1151
Gajoen Kanko Hotel	Tel. (03)3491-0111
Ginza Daiichi Hotel	Tel. (03)3542-5311
Ginza Nikko Hotel	Tel. (03)3571-4911
Ginza Tokyu Hotel	Tel. (03)3541-2411
Haneda Tokyu Hotel	Tel. (03)3747-0311
Hotel Century Hyatt	Tel. (03)3349-0111
Hotel Kokusai Kanko	Tel. (03)3215-3281
Hotel New Otani	Tel. (03)3265-1111
Hotel Okura	Tel. (03)3582-0111
Hotel Pacific Tokyo	Tel. (03)3445-6711
Imperial Hotel	Tel. (03)3504-1111
Keio Plaza Hotel	Tel. (03)3344-0111
Marunouchi Hotel	Tel. (03)3215-2151
Miyako Hotel Tokyo	Tel. (03)3447-3111
Palace Hotel	Tel. (03)3211-5211
Shiba Park Hotel	Tel. (03)3433-4141
Takanawa Prince Hotel	Tel. (03)3447-1111
Takanawa Tobu Hotel	Tel. (03)3447-0111
Tokyo Hilton Hotel	Tel. (03)3344-5111
Tokyo Hotel Urashima	Tel. (03)3533-3111

- LICHEN FLORA of JAPAN
- NATURALIZED PLANTS of JAPAN
- DISEASES and PESTS of CULTIVATED TREES and SHRUBS
- DISEASES and PESTS of FLOWERS and VEGETABLES
- Coloured Guide of Wild Herbs with Artifical Key to Their Families
- THE NEW ALPINE FLORA of JAPAN vol. I
- THE NEW ALPINE FLORA of JAPAN vol. II
- THE LAND SNAILS of JAPAN
- JAPANESE CRUSTACEAN DECAPODS and STOMATOPODS vol. I
- JAPANESE CRUSTACEAN DECAPODS and STOMATOPODS vol. II
- THE LIFE HISTORIES OF BUTTERFLIES IN JAPAN vol. I
- THE LIFE HISTORIES OF BUTTERFLIES IN JAPAN vol. II
- THE LIFE HISTORIES OF BUTTERFLIES IN JAPAN vol. III
- THE LIFE HISTORIES OF BUTTERFLIES IN JAPAN vol. IV
- THE COLEOPTERA OF JAPAN vol. I
- THE COLEOPTERA OF JAPAN vol. II
- THE COLEOPTERA OF JAPAN vol. III
- THE COLEOPTERA OF JAPAN vol. IV
- Colored Illustrations of The Marine Fishes of Japan Vol. I
- Colored Illustrations of The Marine Fishes of Japan Vol. II
- SPIDERS OF JAPAN IN COLOR
- Colored Illustrations of Mushrooms of Japan Vol. I
- Colored Illustrations of Mushrooms of Japan Vol. II
- Ornamental Tropical Plants of the World Vol. I

⟨ NEW COLOR PICTURES ⟩

Book Size 7″ × 10″

Guide to Seashore Animals of Japan with Color Pictures and Keys, Vol. I

Guide to Seashore Animals of Japan with Color Pictures and Keys, Vol. II

The Encyclopedia of Wakan-yaku (Traditionals Sino-Japanese Medicines) with Color Pictures Vol. I, II

Bird's Life in Japan with Color Pictures

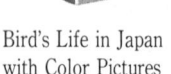

Bird's of mountain, woodland and field

Bird's of marsh, shore and ocean